ACTS
The Gospel throughout the World

You will receive power when the Holy Spirit comes on you;
and you will be My witnesses in Jerusalem, and in all Judea and Samaria,
and to the ends of the earth.
Acts 1:8

Edited by Lois M. Engfehr

CPH
SAINT LOUIS

Series editors: Thomas J. Doyle and Rodney L. Rathmann

Assistant to the editors: Cynthia Anderson

We solicit your comments and suggestions concerning this material. Please write to Product Manager, Adult Bible Studies, Concordia Publishing House, 3558 S. Jefferson Avenue, St. Louis, MO 63118-3968.

Unless otherwise stated, Scripture taken from the HOLY BIBLE, NEW INTERNATIONAL VERSION ®. Copyright © 1973, 1978, 1984 by International Bible Society. Used by permission of Zondervan Publishing House. All rights reserved.

Scripture quotations marked RSV are from the Revised Standard Version of the Bible, copyrighted 1946, 1952, © 1971, 1973. Used by permission.

Scripture quotations marked KJV are from the King James or Authorized Version of the Bible.

Contents

April 27

Lesson 1

The Church Is Born
(Acts 1–2)

Theme Verse

"You will receive power when the Holy Spirit comes on you; and you will be My witnesses in Jerusalem, and in all Judea and Samaria, and to the ends of the earth" **(Acts 1:8).**

Goal

In this lesson we will discover in Acts the nature and purpose of the church as God Himself designed it, and evaluate our own church life in the light of this discovery.

What's Going On Here?

Luke, whom Paul calls "the beloved physician," is the undisputed author of Acts. He had already written a book, the gospel of Luke, which was addressed to a fellow Gentile believer named Theophilus. There, in the first verses, Luke explained that he wished to give an orderly and detailed account of Jesus' earthly life so that Theophilus would have a clear picture of the one in whom he had placed his hope **(Luke 1:1–4).**

Acts takes up where the gospel of Luke leaves off. Once again the book is directed to Theophilus. Luke begins this writing by saying that in his "former book" he had given an account of "all that Jesus began to do and to teach until the day he was taken up to heaven" **(Acts 1:1–2).** In other words, Jesus' earthly life, including His resurrection and ascension, was only the beginning of His work on earth.

This leads into the main truth underlying the book of Acts: Although no longer present in bodily form, Jesus continues His teaching and ministry on earth through His mystical body, the church. This has led one Bible scholar to suggest that a more accurate title for the book would be "The book of the continued doing and teaching of the living Christ by the Holy Spirit through His body which is the church." Acts reveals the very purpose of God in establishing the church and gives the process and power by which He plans to accomplish it.

It is a remarkable thing that Christ has made the completion of His mission work on earth dependent on His body, the church. It is the instrument through which His Spirit moves forward in salvation and on to the final victory described in Revelation. If we as the church are failing to live up to the standard set forth in Acts, we are doing nothing less than hindering the coming of the Kingdom. May God use these studies to renew us and to bring us to a higher level of commitment concerning His plans and purposes for His church.

Searching the Scriptures

1. Read all of **Acts 1–2**.

2. For what purposes did Jesus remain on earth for 40 days following His resurrection according to **Acts 1:2–3?**

3. Compare **Acts 1:3–5** with **Luke 24:36–49**. How are the two accounts similar? different? What special instruction is recorded in both **Luke 24:49** and **Acts 1:4?**

4. When Jesus gave His followers instructions to wait in Jerusalem for the promised "gift" of the Holy Spirit, how did they react **(1:6)?** What was their main concern? How did it correspond with Jesus' main interest **(vv. 7–8)?**

5. Observe **Acts 1:8** carefully. *It is the key verse in Acts.* In it Luke gives us a capsule outline of the whole book. According to what geographic pattern was the Christian witness to advance? What does this key passage reveal about the nature and purpose of the church?

6. How is the Second Coming of Christ described in **verse 11?**

7. Peter indicates the necessity of finding a replacement for Judas. What were the necessary credentials for this man **(1:21–22)?** How does this coincide with the claim made by John in **1 John 1:1?** We have just observed in **Acts 1:8** that this is a book about testifying about Jesus—His person and work. To what specifically was the 12th apostle to have been witness **(1:22)?**

8. On what particular day were the disciples gathered together according to **2:1?** How many days after Ascension would this be?

9. What two external phenomena signaled the outpouring of the Holy Spirit?

10. What precisely did being filled with the Holy Spirit enable believers to do on this occasion (2:4)? What does "speaking in other tongues" mean according to **verse 6?** What was the message the believers were giving as they spoke in other languages (**v. 11**)?

11. How did the Holy Spirit use the supernatural phenomena of Pentecost to gain a hearing for the witness of the believers (**2:6–11**)?

Note: With the coming of the Holy Spirit on the day of Pentecost, the church is born. Observe that the first official activity of the church is the preaching of a sermon to a huge audience. This sermon, delivered by Peter, falls into three main parts: (a) an explanation of what is happening (**2:14–21**); (b) proclaiming the Gospel message of the life, death, resurrection, and ascension of Christ (**2:22–36**); and (c) the exhortation to repent and be baptized (**2:38–40**).

12. Peter explains the occurrences of Pentecost by referring to a prophecy in Joel which predicts the outpouring of the Holy Spirit on all humankind. Why would this particular crowd relate to an Old Testament prophecy (**2:5**)?

13. Peter goes on to say that the supernatural happenings on this day are the beginning of the final age prophesied in Joel. How is this final age designated in **2:17?** How does Joel's message about the "last days" apply to us (**2:20**)?

14. To what does Peter give witness in **2:32?** In whose power does he do this? Refer to the key text, **Acts 1:8.** How does Peter's boldness here compare with his denial of Christ before the crucifixion? See **Luke**

22:54–62. What makes the difference?

15. Peter devotes one verse to the life of Christ **(2:22)**, one to His death **(2:23)**, and nine to His resurrection **(2:24–32)**. Why is the resurrection of such great importance in the Christian witness? See **1 Corinthians 15:14.**

16. How did Peter reply to the question of the crowd, "What shall we do?" in **2:38?** Define the word *repent* using either a standard dictionary or Bible dictionary. What two things result from true repentance according to **2:38?**

17. In the final verses of **Acts 2,** the Holy Spirit offers us a glimpse of how the newborn church functioned. Describe the four vital aspects of body life listed in **2:42.**

18. The life of the church was evident not only in formal religious settings; it spilled over into everyday living. List the attitudes and characteristics of the church as they are described in **2:43–47.**

19. What was the natural result of this dynamic community and who was responsible for this result **(2:47b)?**

The Word for Us

1. When Christ instructed His followers to remain in Jerusalem and await the power they would receive from the Holy Spirit, they did not seem to understand (**1:6–7**). Consequently, they tried to direct Jesus' attention to something of intense concern to themselves. Like all Jews, they anxiously awaited the deliverance of the nation of Israel from Roman domination and the establishment of the Messiah's earthly kingdom. They hoped Jesus' reference to the coming Holy Spirit might mean the dawn of this kingdom.

Jesus did not rebuke His followers for asking this question, nor did He deny the eventual coming of the Kingdom. Instead, He gently redirected their attention to the work which lay before them and the power in which they would perform it.

In what situations in the church today or in your personal life are the directives of Christ being ignored? When do we turn a deaf ear to the Spirit's "nudgings" and make an effort instead to divert His attention to the things that are important to us—our "pet" plans, programs, interests? Even in spiritual matters, we may find ourselves appealing to Him to bless our own desires rather than seeking His will and yielding to it. Discuss with the group the results of such detours.

2. Confessing the life, death, and resurrection of Jesus Christ is the most essential activity of the church. As an individual member of the body of Christ, you testify to the power of Christ in your life. Who empowers you to witness Jesus as He did the first believers? When you do witness, what is the focus of your message? What do you talk about? How do you find and present a Scriptural basis for what you say? If you consider your life a witness, what message are you giving?

3. The outpouring of the Holy Spirit which inaugurated the church is often sought as an emotional experience by Christians today. Now that the church, the body of Christ, has been established, how does a person receive the Holy Spirit according to **1 Corinthians 12:13**? How many believers have received the Holy Spirit? Read **Romans 8:9**.

What does **Ephesians 5:18b** tell Christians to seek? How does the Holy Spirit fill us? What else might be filling us? How does God empty us so that the Spirit of God may fill us? See **Psalm 51:10–12.** What according to **Galatians 5:22–23** is the true evidence (fruit) of being filled with the Spirit?

Closing

Pray together the following stanzas of "The Church's One Foundation."

The Church's one foundation
    Is Jesus Christ, her Lord;
She is His new creation
    By water and the Word.
From heav'n He came and sought her
    To be His holy bride;
With His own blood He bought her,
    And for her life He died.

 Elect from ev'ry nation,
    Yet one o'er all the earth;
Her charter of salvation:
    One Lord, one faith, one birth.
One holy name she blesses,
    Partakes one holy food,
And to one hope she presses
    With ev'ry grace endued.

To Do This Week

Read through the entire book of Acts. Then reread **Acts 3:1–4:31** in preparation for the next lesson.

Lesson 2

May 4

The Infant Church Acts
(Acts 3:1–4:31)

Theme Verse

"Salvation is found in no one else, for there is no other name under heaven given to men by which we must be saved" **(Acts 4:12).**

Goal

In this lesson we will identify the ongoing work of the church following Pentecost, seek to understand the nature of the opposition which inevitably confronts this work, and recognize the source of the church's power to withstand opposition and persist in its kingdom-building activity.

What's Going On Here?

In **Acts 2** Luke gave us a thrilling account of the birth of the church on Pentecost Sunday. Imagine for a moment what the Monday after must have been like. Even in our personal lives we may experience spiritual "highs" on Sunday, but when Monday comes with its nagging everyday demands and conflicts, the bubble is burst. We're back in the pressure cooker of the "real" world. Yet our daily stresses must be small in comparison to the monumental problems which confronted the newborn church. Its leaders, the 12 apostles, were not from Jerusalem; yet this was the place God had appointed for the establishing and launching of His work. The Twelve were not to return to their homes and occupations in Galilee. They were to remain in Jerusalem, carry on their witness, and minister to the some 3,000 converts, nurturing them to maturity before sending them back to their homelands.

What an assignment! Remaining in Jerusalem posed practical problems of mammoth proportions.

The church was almost 100% Jewish at this point. Undoubtedly some of the new converts were from Jerusalem. While they could help with housing, it was impossible for them to take the whole assembly under their roofs. This need gave rise to an incredible strategy. With united hearts, responding to the love of God, these first believers voluntarily sold "their possessions and goods [and] they gave to anyone as he had need" **(Acts 2:45)**. There is no evidence here of a permanent communal living arrangement. Other local churches, for example, those established in Ephesus, Galatia, and Philippi, did not adopt communal patterns. This was a stopgap measure necessitated by the unique circumstances in Jerusalem. Property was sold and money was pooled to rent homes and apartments and to provide food and necessities for those who had no source of income. Thus, in its earliest stages, the fellowship of the church encompassed the whole of everyday living.

Believers also continued to meet in the temple, not to take part in Jewish worship, but to assemble for instruction by the apostles. The temple courts were a place of constant coming and going. They were filled with the bleating of sheep, the calls of the moneychangers, and the lively activities of Levites, priests, and teachers. Thus, the whole church could not possibly assemble there at one time. Instead, the apostles probably made themselves available for teaching all day long in an area along one side of the temple wall called Solomon's Colonnade. It can be assumed that they followed the pattern of the rabbis and gathered small groups around themselves at various times during the day to ground them in a knowledge of Jesus and of His teaching. In its early stages, then, the church split into smaller congregations which met in the temple during the day for teaching. In the evening the believers retired to their assigned homes to share a life of worship, prayer, and fellowship.

These circumstances shed light on the description of the early fellowship in **Acts 2:42–47,** and they also prepare us for the setting which we encounter in the third and fourth chapters of Acts. This is the first picture of the church as it is to be, as a result of the tongues of fire and the enthusiasm of Pentecost. We see now that those "mountaintop" experiences would prepare the church for real-life situations. We find that the continuous and normal activity of the church is in the commonplaces of life and among the cripples. The church is filled with the Spirit so that it may go into the world to meet people's needs, including their greatest need—forgiveness of sins and eternal life.

Searching the Scriptures

1. Read all of **Acts 3:1–4:31.**

2. Summarize the healing of the man crippled from birth recounted in **Acts 3:1–10.** This is a dramatic account. Like a playwright, Luke gives the time, setting, and main characters in **verses 1–2.** What and who are they? What other noteworthy details does Luke offer?

3. In what way does the miraculous healing here function exactly as the miracle of other languages in **2:11?**

4. How does Peter explain the healing **(v. 16)?** How might the healing have been misinterpreted according to **verse 12?**

5. Compare the main thrusts of Peter's sermon in **verses 12–26** with his first sermon in **2:22–39.** List the similarities. How does this repetition reinforce the truths we have been discovering as to the essential witness of the church?

6. How does Peter relate the message of Christ specifically to the Jews in **verses 17–26?** To whom was the message of salvation to be extended first **(v. 26)?** How does this fit in with the master plan outlined by Jesus in **Acts 1:8?** See also **Matthew 10:5–8.**

7. Who was disturbed by Peter's message? What precisely disturbed them (4:1–2)?

8. What were the two results of Peter's second sermon recorded in verses 3 and 4?

9. How would you characterize the group of people before whom Peter and John had to appear (v. 5)? How does their background compare with that of the two disciples according to verse 13? Which of these two groups, the disciples or their investigators, would be considered by the world to have the greater power?

10. By whose power is Peter able to confront this imposing group of men (v. 10)? See also Luke 12:11–12. How does this power continue to enable, strengthen, and motivate Christians today?

11. Not only do miracles provide occasion for witness, opposition serves the same purpose! In response to the interrogation of the rulers, Peter takes the opportunity to give a bold testimony of Christ. What again is the focal point of his witness in verses 10 and 12? How might God use occasions for opposition or trouble today as an opportunity for a Christian to testify to Christ?

12. Why is it impossible for the religious leaders to refute what Peter has said **(vv. 14** and **16)?** Why did these learned men ignore the miracle? See **John 5:40.**

13. How do Peter and John reply to their threats **(vv. 18–20)?**

14. What action does the church take in response to the opposition of the religious rulers **(v. 24)?** What is the result? In what ways is their prayer immediately answered **(vv. 29–31)?**

15. What is the external evidence of being "filled with the Holy Spirit" in **verse 31?** How did the Holy Spirit manifest Himself in the fellowship of believers **(vv. 31–32)?**

The Word for Us

1. Consider again the healing of the crippled man. Compare it with specific miracles performed by Christ? See **Mark 2:1–12** and **John 5:1–15.** How does this emphasize once more the exciting truth that Christ continues to work on earth in and through the church? What is His ministry to the world as illustrated in the healing of the man crippled from birth and Peter's subsequent sermon?

When is it dangerous for the church to put too much emphasis on miraculous signs? What is the purpose of these signs as stated in **John 11:4** and **Mark 16:20?** See Peter's explanation **(Acts 3:16)**. Look at Jesus' rebuke against those who seek after a sign in **Matthew 12:39.** What is wrong with seeking after signs?

How does the church still offer healing to a world in dire need of it? Consider physical, emotional, and spiritual healing in your discussion.

2. The Sadducees were a sect of the Jews that did not accept the supernatural. They did not believe in the Spirit, in angels, or in the resurrection from the dead. How does this help explain their vehement reaction to Peter's testimony in **Acts 4:2?** Of what does Jesus accuse the Sadducees in **Matthew 22:29?** What views in the church today remind you of the approach of the Sadducees to the portions of Scripture which contain references to the supernatural?

3. Note the number of times the "name of Jesus" is referred to in these chapters **(Acts 3:6, 16; 4:7, 10, 12, 17, 18, 30)**. This is clearly a key phrase. What does it mean that the church functions "in the name of Jesus"? What does it mean to pray "in the name of Jesus"? How much power does the name of Jesus actually carry according to **Matthew 28:18?** In addition to this tremendous power, what responsibilities does bearing this name imply?

4. Peter and John took time to look carefully at the beggar (**Acts 3:4**). They did not brush him off with a quick handout. What about the people you encounter in the day-to-day activities of your life? Are you grasping the opportunity to expose them to the healing that Christ has to offer? While we may not be able to enter the foreign mission field, God in His wisdom brings the mission field to us. What about the homeless and the mentally ill? Sometimes they are treated as the weak and despised elements in our society. We must be willing to meet each and every individual with God's love right where he or she is, just as Jesus met the woman at the well in **John 4:1–42.** Who is sitting at the doorstep of your life right now, needing to know the healing power of the Lord?

Closing

Sing or speak together the following stanza of "Today Your Mercy Calls Us."

Today Your mercy calls us
    To wash away our sin.
However great our trespass,
    Whatever we have been,
However long from mercy
    Our hearts have turned away,
Your precious blood can wash us
    And make us clean today.

To Do This Week

Read **Acts 4:32–5:42** in preparation for the next class session. Begin each day "in the name of Jesus" as you ask that the Holy Spirit would empower you to witness boldly God's love for you in Christ Jesus by your words and through your actions.

Lesson 3 *May 11*

Growing Pains
(Acts 4:32–5:42)

Theme Verse

"Peter and the other apostles replied: 'We must obey God rather than men!' " **(Acts 5:29).**

Goal

In this lesson we will learn how the infant church by the power of the Holy Spirit confronted perils within and without, and examine perils that we may encounter in our present-day church experience and confront them as we are empowered by the Holy Spirit working through God's Word.

What's Going On Here?

When the lame man begged alms from Peter at the Beautiful Gate, Peter responded with, "Silver or gold I do not have." This lack of material possessions characterized the first-century church as well as the personal lives of the apostles. Their passion was not for material possessions, but for Christ instead. This is why the first believers could so trustfully deposit their wealth "at the apostles' feet." They knew the hearts of the apostles—that they had no taste for material things, that they would never use the offerings for personal luxuries but would distribute the money to the church community as there was need.

While the communal living necessitated in the first years of the church was a passing phenomenon, the standard of utter abandonment of all that we are and have to the purposes of God is an attitude of heart that we embrace as the Spirit strengthens our faith. The question is not "Should we live in communes?" but "Would we be willing to give up all our possessions at a moment's notice?" Is your heart primarily attached to the things of this earth or to God?

It is clear also from the makeup of the early church that God does not dwell in buildings made by human hands. Before there were buildings or committees or boards there was church life, body life. Insular Christianity was never in God's plan. The church began as community; that was its essential nature. Its dynamism derived from the fact that all members were filled with the Spirit and all had the unity of love. Furthermore, even though Jesus had commissioned the church to expand its witness to the ends of the earth, there was no worldwide mission program for the first eight years. Even the apostles stayed where they were, in Jerusalem. The responsibility of church members was simply to experience the life of Christ with their brothers and sisters. Just being a part of this exciting church life prepared these early believers for later powerful ministry. In the meantime, they witnessed right where they were.

Luke reports that there was another great influx of converts (Acts 4:4). This phenomenal growth brought with it new financial needs. Once again the church responded spontaneously with individuals selling possessions to meet the needs of others. In Acts 4:36–37 Barnabas is held up as a model for such unselfish giving. His example stands in sharp contrast to the one we encounter at the beginning of chapter 5 when flagrant sin threatens the infant church.

Searching the Scriptures

1. Read all of Acts 4:32–5:42.

2. Review the activities of the church as described in Acts 4:32–37. What was the attitude of these believers and what action did it spontaneously produce? What remained the primary activity of the church (v. 33)?

3. Ananias and Sapphira are counter examples to Barnabas. What exactly was their sin? (See 5:3–4, 7–9.) Who was the instigator of the sin (v. 3)?

4. Why did God respond to this act of sin with such severe judgment?

5. What effect did this episode have on the church (vv. 5, 11)? How does this attitude stand in contrast with that of Ananias and Sapphira? Use **Galatians 6:7** to help with your answer.

6. What does Luke call the assembly of believers for the first time in **verse 11?** What is the significance of this term?

7. What blessing and power flowed from the church once the evil of Ananias and Sapphira had been removed (vv. 12–16)? Discuss the importance of effective church discipline today.

8. How did the Sadducees react to this activity and growth (vv. 17–18)?

9. How were the apostles freed? For what purpose? How did they respond (vv. 19–21a)?

10. Characterize the assembly before which the apostles were summoned (**v. 21b**)? **Note:** The Sanhedrin was the supreme Jewish court composed of 70 to 100 men. It was rare for the whole assembly to meet together. In light of this, what note of humor do you detect in **verses 22–25?**

11. How does the testimony of the high priest in **verse 28** show the impact of Christian teaching?

12. Read again Peter's minisermon in **verses 29–32.** What points does he repeat from his two earlier sermons? Who witnesses with him (**v. 32**)?

13. To whom is the Holy Spirit given according to **verse 32?** How does this echo the response of Peter and the apostles to the high priest in **verse 29?** Obedience is joyful response to God's love in Christ. The church obedient is the church led by God's Spirit at work in and through His Word. What does obedience to God entail for Christians today?

14. Give a thumbnail sketch of Gamaliel (**vv. 33–34**). Who, according to **Acts 22:3,** was one of his pupils? Summarize his cautious recommendation (**vv. 35–39**). Why might Gamaliel's advice be good for us to remember?

15. What gave the apostles cause for rejoicing in **verse 41?** How does

this experience bear out what Jesus had foretold in **Matthew 10:17** and promised in **Luke 6:22–23?**

16. The focus and activity of the church persisted despite internal and external assaults. Give the essential nature and purpose of the church as described in **verses 41–42.**

The Word for Us

1. Compare God's judgment on Ananias and Sapphira with that executed upon the sons of Aaron in **Leviticus 10:1–2.** Taking into consideration the fact that the incident recorded in Leviticus occurred at the inauguration of the priesthood and that the judgment in **Acts 5** takes place at the inauguration of the church age, what is the message God has for us in these accounts? Compare also **Joshua 7:25** and **2 Samuel 6:7.**

2. The story of Ananias and Sapphira carries a deep lesson that applies both to the church and to the individual Christian. The infant church was threatened by a deliberate lie to the Holy Spirit. Ananias's hypocrisy was swept away by an act of swift judgment. Note how the early church was learning to fear and trust God above all things **(vv. 5–6).**

What is the environment within our churches today? Are there attempts to lie to the Holy Spirit? Are we allowing the things of the world into our fellowship, compromising the high ideals of our most holy God? Is church discipline weak these days? What can be done to improve evangelical church discipline?

What about our own lives? Do we allow dishonesty of any sort? Do we indulge in pretense? Are we guilty of hypocrisy when we sing hymns and anthems of total consecration to Christ, yet live lives which are at best spiritually lukewarm? May God enable us to confess all that is pretense, selfishness, and hypocrisy in our lives! Use **Psalm 15** and **51** to pray that God would help you to search your heart and remove all that is impure.

3. Note again the attitude of joy in suffering expressed by the apostles in **Acts 5:41.** Read **1 Peter 4:12–19** for a more detailed account of how a Christian is to respond to suffering. When do you experience ridicule because of your devotion to Jesus—at work, in your community, even in your home? What special encouragement have you received from God's Word today?

4. We have studied enough in Acts to understand that the church of Jesus Christ is involved in testifying to Him. In that one word is condensed the whole wisdom of God as to the worldwide work which He would have His people accomplish in this age. As a member of the church, how are you testifying to Jesus Christ?

Look at Peter's testimony in **Acts 5:30–32.** Who is witnessing along with Peter? This should be a source of tremendous encouragement to us as we carry out Christ's command to tell the world of Him. Read **John 15:26–27** and discuss this partnership. What is my part? What is the Holy Spirit's part?

Closing

Speak or sing together the following stanzas from "Jesus, Your Blood and Righteousness."

Jesus, Your blood and righteousness
My beauty are, my glorious dress;
Mid flaming worlds, in these arrayed,
With joy shall I lift up my head.

Bold shall I stand in that great day,
Cleansed and redeemed, no debt to pay:
For by Your cross absolved I am
From sin and guilt, from fear and shame.

To Do This Week

Reread the portions of the book of **Acts** studied this far. Then read **Acts 6–7** in preparation for the next class session.

Lesson 4

May 18

Marks of Maturity
(Acts 6–7)

Theme Verse

"But they could not stand up against his wisdom or the Spirit by whom he spoke" **(Acts 6:10).**

Goal

In this lessson we will see in the example of Stephen that the church and its individual members can encounter the deadliest attack and emerge victorious through faith in Christ Jesus.

What's Going On Here?

During His earthly ministry, Jesus made a single but highly significant reference to the church, the universal body of believers. It is recorded in the gospel of Matthew. After He had spent some time with His 12 disciples, teaching them, demonstrating His power through miracles, and sharing His life with them, Jesus asked pointedly, "Who do you say that I am?" It was Simon to whom the truth of Jesus' divine person had been revealed. With characteristic eagerness, he responded, "You are the Christ, the Son of the living God" **(Matthew 16:16).** Jesus blessed Simon for this inspired answer, and then symbolically changed Simon's name to Peter which is derived from the Greek word for "rock." Jesus continued by saying, "On this rock I will build my church, and the gates of Hades will not overcome it" **(Matthew 16:18).**

As we have studied Acts, we have seen a fulfillment of this promise. In all his preaching and evangelizing, Peter, the undisputed leader in the early church, reiterates the bold confession he made that day in Caesarea Philippi: "Jesus is the Christ, the Messiah! Jesus is the Son of God!" It is upon the "rock" of that confession that the Holy Spirit built the church. We have observed how its numbers and its impact grew by leaps and bounds.

There was fierce opposition, of course, as we have seen. Jesus alluded to the inevitability of this when He gave the assurance that all the powers of hell would not prevail against His church. In the chapters before us we will see a vivid fulfillment of this prediction when fiendish forces lash out against the church. Stephen is viciously attacked, but, in this first martyr, we have a most wonderful confirmation of God's intervention in the lives of His saints. Even in death, Stephen, not his assailants, is the real victor. Praise God!

As you read chapter 6 of Acts, bear in mind that the church at this point was still composed almost entirely of Jews. There were, however, two distinct groups: (1) Hebraic Jews who still lived in the land of Judah and held strictly to the Hebrew language and customs; and (2) Hellenistic Jews who were born outside of Palestine and had adopted the Greek language, attitudes, and customs. This will help explain the new problem which arises in the church as the scene opens.

Searching the Scriptures

1. Read all of **Acts 6** and **7.**

2. Study **Acts 6:1.** What problem is described? What positive circumstances within the church gave rise to this problem? Compare the conflict of these two groups with a modern-day division that could occur in a congregation or community.

3. What two ministries of the church are listed in **verse 2?** Compare the importance of the two. Note the qualifications of the seven men in **verses 3** and **5** to help you with your answer.

4. What importance did the apostles attach to this issue (**vv. 2–6**)? How soon after the problem was brought to their attention do you think they took action? What "marks of maturity" accompany their response? What was the result (**v. 7**)?

5. Who chose "the seven" (**vv. 3, 5**)? Who ordained them (**v. 6**)?

6. All seven names listed in **verse 5** are Greek. Discuss the wisdom of this solution. Charles Spurgeon once commented, "If you have an angular, peculiar person in your church, always put him in office and keep him at work." Discuss this quote with your group as it relates to the issue at hand.

7. How is Stephen characterized in **verses 5, 8,** and **10**? What are his "marks of maturity?" Keep looking for these as you continue in the study.

8. Explain how Stephen could do that which only the apostles had done up to this time (**vv. 6, 8**).

9. When actual good is being done in the world by the church and its members, there will be opposition. Who opposed Stephen (**v. 9**)? Why could no one refute him (**v. 10**)? How did this fulfill the promise in **Luke 21:15?** How can you claim this promise for yourself?

10. Summarize the accusations against Stephen **(vv. 11, 13–14)**. What similarities do you note between this situation and the trial of Jesus in **Mark 14:55–60?**

11. Describe the scene in which Stephen is confronted by the power figures of the day, i.e., the Sanhedrin **(v. 15)**. Who obviously has the upper hand? See **2 Corinthians 3:18** to observe how Stephen's experience is in keeping with God's design for His people. You are included! How is God transforming your life into the likeness of Christ?

12. Speaking in response to the accusations against him, Stephen reviews the history of the Hebrew nation beginning with the call of Abraham and continuing to the building of the temple by Solomon **(7:1–50)**. Identify the main themes.

13. At first glance it may seem that Stephen is trying to conciliate his accusers by identifying with them and recounting their common history. In **7:51–53** the tone changes abruptly. Who is the accuser? Is Stephen foolhardy or courageous?

14. Reread **verses 51–53.** Were Stephen's listeners circumcised physically? In what sense were they uncircumcised? Compare with situations that could occur or have occurred in the church. When are we tempted to be stiff-necked and uncircumcised in hearts and ears?

15. Review the account of Stephen's death in **verses 54–60.** Which details remind you of Christ's death? What similarities do you see between Jesus and Stephen? What conclusions can you draw from this concerning the secret of Stephen's spiritual maturity? See **Philippians 3:7–10.**

16. Note the vicious reaction to Stephen's mention of angels and of heaven in **verses 53–57.** This crowd was composed largely of Sadducees. How does this shed light on their frenzied reaction?

17. Who was present in the crowd? What was his contribution and his attitude toward the stoning **(7:58; 8:1)?**

The Word for Us

1. In **Acts 6** we have the first instance of organization within the church. How did it come about? What ecclesiastical details indicate that the "office" created here is fixed in the life of the church? What is primary in the working of the church? Are some jobs to be considered more important than others?

2. The peace exhibited by Stephen, the child of God, stands in glaring contrast with the turmoil of his fiendish opponents. Now consider yourself and the circumstances which presently face you. Can they be any more ominous than the dark powers which threatened Stephen? Can God give you peace in your circumstances? Read and memorize **Isaiah 26:3.**

Discuss with your group ways of living in closer personal union with Christ. This was the key to Stephen's maturity. How does God mold you to the image of Christ through the trials in your life?

3. Stephen was a layman, yet he was exceptionally mature in the faith and well-versed in Scripture. There were as yet no seminaries or Bible colleges. How do you suppose Stephen attained such spiritual stature? See **Ephesians 4:16.** How do we? Why is a person who is mightily used of the Lord also actively involved in the corporate life of the church? When are people mightily used by the Lord though not in the professional ministry? How can you be mightily used by the Lord? How may this Bible study of Acts help?

4. Read **2 Timothy 3:10–15.** Discuss why people who begin to live a life truly consecrated to the Lord often experience added trials? Compare Satan's attitude toward a believer who does little more than "warm the pew" on Sunday mornings to his attitude toward a believer who is a bold witness to Christ.

Would you be willing to die for Christ? The Greek word for "witness" is the same as the word for "martyr." To witness in Stephen's day often meant to die. Although we may not be called upon to give up our physical lives for Christ, there are other "dyings" involved in witnessing for Him. Name some. Are you willing to suffer them for Christ's sake? What reassurance do you receive from the account of Stephen's death? What special grace did God grant him?

Closing

Speak or sing together this stanza of "Let Us Ever Walk with Jesus."

Let us ever walk with Jesus,
    Follow His cxample pure,
Through a world that would deceive us
    And to sin our spirits lure.
Onward in His footsteps treading,
    Pilgrims here, our home above,
Full of faith and hope and love,
    Let us do our Father's bidding,
    Faithful Lord, with me abide;
I shall follow where You guide.

To Do This Week

Review the questions from "The Word for Us." Pray that the Holy Spirit might use you to serve God. Read **Acts 8–9** in preparation for the next class session.

May 26

Lesson 5

Thrust Out of the Nest
(Acts 8–9)

Theme Verse

"Those who had been scattered preached the word wherever they went" **(Acts 8:4).**

Goal

In this lesson we will discover how God faithfully activated His plan for the extension of the church beyond Jerusalem.

What's Going On Here?

Chapter 8 brings us to a turning point in Acts. It marks the second major division of the book, based on the master plan outlined in **1:8b:** "You will be my witnesses in Jerusalem, and in all Judea and Samaria, and to the ends of the earth." In chapters 1 through 7 we have observed how the church carried out its witness to Christ in Jerusalem. Now we come to the work of the Holy Spirit through His disciples in the regions of Judea and Samaria. We also discover the seeds of His work beyond these realms. Examine the chart below to gain an understanding of the movement of **Acts** from beginning to end.

The Early Church

Chapters 1–7	Chapters 8–12	Chapters 13–28
Jerusalem	*Judea and Samaria*	*Ends of the Earth*
Jewish Period	Transition	Gentile Period
Church Established	Church Scattered	Church Extended
1–2 Church Born	**8–9** Church Sent Abroad	**13–21** Church Extends Overseas
3–7 Church Grows	**10–12** Church Embraces Gentiles	**22–28** Church Leaders on Trial

The expansion of the church beyond Jerusalem into Judea was a natural development. Jewish Christians first shared the Good News with their fellow citizens. The ministry to the Samaritans was a more complicated matter. We know from the account of Jesus at the well of Sychar in **John 4** that Jews did not associate with Samaritans (**v. 9**). Samaria, the name given to the northern kingdom of Israel, was populated, not by Jews, but by a people of mixed ancestry. See **2 Kings 17.** They adopted the teachings of Moses but set up their own temple. They identified sacred places within their own country. As a result, Jews of the Southern Kingdom (Judah) regarded them with contempt. Jesus, we know, ignored such ethnic and religious prejudice and gave Himself to all in need. The church, as the instrument of His purposes on earth, does the same. It transcends all barriers of culture, geography, and race and offers the saving Gospel to all who will receive it. This is clearly evidenced in the chapters before us.

Chapter 7 closed with an awesome scene. It featured two young men with an amazing influence on the early church. While the one, Stephen, was being stoned to death, the other, Saul, was in the cheering section at this execution. Stephen was an elder in the church; Saul was a Pharisee, well-acquainted with the religious leaders of Jerusalem and hostile to the new church and to Stephen. In the murder of Stephen, the Sanhedrin (the governing body of Jewish religious leaders) silenced a voice that was upsetting a city; yet in Saul, the Holy Spirit was at work, awakening a new voice that would upset an empire.

Searching the Scriptures

1. Read **Acts 8** and **9.**

2. What seemingly negative circumstance did God use to accomplish His strategy for expansion into Judea and Samaria (**8:1**)?

3. What did the scattered Christians do according to **verse 4?** Note that the word *scattered* in this verse is an agricultural term for the sowing or broadcasting of seed. How does this imagery enhance your appreciation of what God is accomplishing through His people? Read **Matthew 13:37–38**

to see how this description of witnessing Christians corresponds to Jesus' imagery.

4. What was Philip, by the power of the Holy Spirit, able to do which authenticated his ministry and opened the way for the proclamation of the Gospel (vv. 6–7)?

5. Review the account of Simon the sorcerer in **verses 9–13** and **18–24.** Scholars are not in agreement as to whether Simon was saved. Which facts from the text would argue for his faith and which would argue against it? The sin of simony derives its name from this man. What is it? Are there any "Simons" on the religious scene today?

6. Reread **8:14–17.** Who were sent to Samaria and what did they do? What was the result of their action? What do you think Simon was able to observe in **verse 18?**

7. Review the account of the Ethiopian eunuch in **verses 26–40.** Why were no signs needed to set the stage for the presentation of the Gospel here? Who is obviously at work preparing the heart of both student and teacher?

8. Summarize the story of Saul's conversion in your own words (**9:1–19**). Note that Paul himself retells the story in **Acts 22:4–16** where several details not found in this account are included.

9. In what sense had Saul been persecuting Jesus (**vv. 4–5**)? What assurance concerning the church do we receive from this insight?

10. Who did God appoint to lay hands on Saul so that he might receive his sight and be filled with the Spirit (**vv. 10–11**)? Does the text indicate that there was anything extraordinary about this man? What does this tell you about the Lord's methods in accomplishing His work?

11. What did Saul do immediately following his Baptism which is a mark of true conversion (**vv. 20, 28**)? What was the content of his preaching (**vv. 20, 22?**)

12. Read **9:23** in the light of **Galatians 1:17–18.** How long was "many days" and where did Saul spend a part of this time? What do you suppose he did there?

13. What conditions named in **Acts 9:31** are evidences of a healthy church?

14. Peter too was involved in missionary endeavors outside Jerusalem. What two notable miracles did he perform (vv. 32–41)? Of which two miracles of Jesus do these remind us?

15. What was Dorcas' gift? How was it a spiritual gift? See **Romans 12:6–8.** Why is such a gift important in the church today?

The Word for Us

1. "If anyone does not have the Spirit of Christ, he does not belong to Christ" **(Romans 8:9).** This and other New Testament texts **(1 John 4:13; 1 Corinthians 12:3, 13)** make clear that every believer has the Spirit of Christ. Yet the Samaritans who had believed Philip's message and were baptized did not "receive the Holy Spirit" until the apostles laid hands on them. How can these seemingly contradictory facts be reconciled?

2. Compare Saul's personality before his conversion **(Acts 8:1, 3)** with that evidenced in **9:20, 28, 29.** How did his personality change? How are Saul's words in **9:5** a testimony of this inner change? How does **2 Corinthians 5:17** describe what has happened to Saul? How do you live under the management of Christ? How do you surrender your character traits to the Lord so that He can use you as He used Saul?

3. Compare the reception of the Gospel in Simon with that of the Ethiopian eunuch. How does the parable of the sower help you to understand the contrasting reactions **(Matthew 13)?** What particularly intrigued Simon and how did this fit in with his past **(8:13)?** What, in contrast, captured the Ethiopian's attention and how did this fit in with what we learn of him from **8:27?**

What are some indications that even today people adopt the external trappings of religion without yielding to the Holy Spirit's power in their lives? When do we become racketeers who attempt to secure spiritual power for personal gain?

4. Most Christians today have referred the task of sharing the Gospel to the professionals, but it is clear from this study that God's master strategy in the church is to have each and every Christian involved in this task. The believers who were scattered in **Acts 8:1** were Christians like you and me. We all have the responsibility of telling others about Jesus.

God used Philip to win souls. Think of his qualifications as they are implied or stated in **Acts 6:3** and **8:4–40.** Charles Spurgeon suggested these lists of Godward and manward traits in the effective soul-winner. Use them to measure your own life. Ask God to supply those qualifications which you find are lacking.

Godward: holiness of character, spiritual life, humility, living faith, earnestness, simplicity of heart, complete surrender.

Manward: knowledge, sincerity, evident earnestness, love, unselfishness, seriousness, tenderness.

Closing

Sing or speak together this stanza of " 'Come, Follow Me' Said Christ, the Lord."

"Come, follow Me," said Christ, the Lord,
    "All in My way abiding;
Your selfishness throw overboard,
    Obey My call and guiding.
Oh, bear your crosses, and confide
    In My example as your guide."

To Do This Week

Read **Acts 10–12** in preparation for the next class session.

Lesson 6

Broadening Horizons
(Acts 10–12)

Theme Verse

"Then Peter began to speak: 'I now realize how true it is that God does not show favoritism but accepts men from every nation who fear Him and do what is right' " (**Acts 10:34–35**).

Goal

In this lesson we will observe the sovereignty of God in the affairs of His church as He (1) opens the door of the Gospel to the Gentile world and (2) perpetuates the spread of the Gospel despite violent political attack. We will also learn from this that God is equally sovereign in the church today.

What's Going On Here?

Chapter 9 of Acts concluded with the report that "Peter stayed in Joppa for some time with a tanner named Simon." This seemingly commonplace detail foreshadows the monumental change in attitude which was to take place within the church. The occupation of the tanner, who handled the "unclean" bodies of dead animals, was contemptible to the Jews. The tanner was required to build his home 75 feet outside the city. Peter's willingness to lodge with a man of this despised trade signals a breaking down of deeply ingrained religious prejudices.

Still, Simon the tanner was at least a Jew. The far more extreme bias which existed in the Jewish mind against Gentiles would be considerably more difficult to overcome. We can scarcely conceive of the psychological barriers many Jews had built up against non-Jews. Gentiles were regarded as filthy and unclean, no better than dogs. The devout Jew thanked God daily that he was not a Gentile. If the shadow of a Gentile fell on a Jew, that Jew had to go to the temple to purify himself.

The extension of the Gospel to Samaritans, who were despised by the Jews, and to the Ethiopian, who was a convert to Judaism, was surprising enough to the early church leaders. The general acceptance of Gentile converts would be a far more drastic step which would rock the church to its center and even threaten to split it in two.

Undoubtedly Peter and the other leaders expected Christianity to remain within the confines of Judaism. Jesus was a Jew, His apostles were Jews, and His earthly ministry had been directed to Jews. His followers, even though they now believed in Him as Savior, still observed Jewish worship and ceremonial customs. To the apostles, Gentiles were still "unclean." Nothing apart from aggressive divine intervention would alter these deeply entrenched habits of thinking.

As the Lord ushered His church into this new phase, two other important shifts took place.

1. The Gentile city of Antioch replaced Jerusalem as the center of Gospel preaching. Located 300 miles north of Jerusalem, Antioch was the third largest city in the Roman Empire and was the Mediterranean doorway to the great eastern highways. It was a city of unspeakable moral decadence and rampant idol worship—quite a training ground for fledgling missionaries. If Saul and Barnabas could succeed in this setting, they could take the Gospel anywhere.

2. Peter, the apostle of the circumcision, passed from the scene in Luke's account, and Paul, the apostle to the Gentiles, took over. Peter, of course, was still active, but he is mentioned only one more time in **Acts 15.**

Searching the Scriptures

1. Read **Acts 10–12.** Note that **11:1–18** is a recapitulation of the account in chapter 10.

2. List the character traits and habitual activities of Cornelius in **10:1–8.** What do these tell you about the condition of his heart? How did Cornelius apparently influence those around him **(vv. 7–8)?**

3. In what respect is Cornelius like the Ethiopian eunuch? What was God's attitude toward Cornelius? See **John 1:4; Luke 8:15.** Was Cornelius saved at this point?

4. Review the details of Peter's trance **(vv. 9–16).** What does it mean? What effect would the threefold repetition have **(Matt. 26:69–75; John 21:15–19)?** Why did God have to be so emphatic? How does Peter's exclamation in **verse 14** indicate that this new idea seems preposterous to him? When does Peter fully understand the vision?

5. Note the precise timing of these remarkable events **(vv. 17–23).** Who was orchestrating this whole affair **(vv. 19–20)?** Would Peter have gone to the Gentiles without divine intervention **(vv. 28–29)?** What action in **verse 23** shows that Peter's prejudice against the Gentiles was beginning to break down?

6. Summarize Peter's message to the Gentiles in **verses 36–43.**

7. What finally and fully convinced Peter that God intended Gentiles to be a part of the body of Christ **(vv. 44–48)?** Who else observed this phenomenon **(v. 45)?** How did this evidence prove indispensable in convincing Jewish Christians in Jerusalem when they challenged Peter's conduct **(11:15–18)?** If Peter and the Jewish leaders refused to accept the Gentiles, whom would they be opposing **(v. 17)?**

8. Review **11:19–30.** How did the church of Antioch come into being? What group made up a large part of its constituency **(v. 20)?** Who was sent to check on this new ministry and what did he observe **(vv. 22–24)?**

9. As you study the Antioch church, list elements of vital Christian fellowship which you find expressed there. How was the new church strengthened **(v. 26)?** The label *Christian* means belonging to Christ. What are the responsibilities of bearing this name? How is the unity of the body beautifully evidenced in this account of the church at Antioch?

10. How did the tragic event reported in **12:1–2** fulfill what Jesus had prophesied to James in **Matthew 20:22–23?** Why would news of this tragedy be particularly disturbing to the church? How did this jolt generate or intensify the activity reported in **Acts 12:5?** How may the intensified prayers of the church be connected with Peter's incredible composure in **verse 6?** When have you experienced a similar inexplicable peace as a result of the prayers of Christian friends? Share with your group.

11. Note the ministry of the angel in Peter's deliverance from prison **(vv. 6–10).** Was Peter aware of what was happening **(v. 9)?** When did the matter become clear in his mind **(vv. 10–11)?** Do angels still minister to believers **(Hebrews 1:14)?**

12. We are told of the earnest prayers of the church. How would you describe these prayers **(vv. 15–16)?** What challenge for your own prayer life do you see in this **(James 1:6)?** Even though these Christians doubted that their prayers would be answered, how did God graciously respond?

13. The Herod of chapter 12 is Herod Agrippa I, nephew of Herod Antipas, who had beheaded John, and grandson of Herod the Great, who had ordered the slaughter of the innocents at the time of Jesus' birth. Herod Agrippa's sudden death is corroborated by the historian Josephus.

What effect did Peter's escape have on Herod **(v. 19)?** How does this show the condition of his heart? What is he obviously denying with this cruel act? How is this attitude further evidenced in the circumstances surrounding Herod's death?

14. How does the simple report in **verse 24** stand in sharp contrast to what Herod, with all his power and the intense evil of his nature, had tried to accomplish? See **verses 1–2.** What message do we get concerning God's power as opposed to all human resources and authority?

The Word for Us

1. The story of Cornelius' conversion is an exciting example of the way in which God supplies truth to those who trust Him. How is this a fulfillment of God's promises in **Deuteronomy 4:29** and **Hebrews 11:6?**

We often are faced with the question, "What about those who have never heard of Christ? Will they too be condemned?" How does the story of Cornelius shed light on this issue? Use **Romans 1:18–20** in your discussion.

2. Peter's presentation of the Gospel to the Gentiles in **Acts 10:34–43** is far more brief than his previous two sermons to Jewish audiences (**Acts 2:14–40; 3:12–26**). What elements does he leave out in addressing Cornelius and his family? What elements remain constant?

Read **1 Corinthians 15:3–7** and list the essential ingredients of the Gospel.

How do **Acts 10:44** and **11:15** indicate that Peter had only begun his sermon to the Gentiles? Who interrupts him (**10:44**)? Who alone can bring people to the point of conversion? By what means does He do so?

3. Even though he was an apostle who was born again and filled with the Spirit, Peter harbored a great deal of prejudice. What areas of your life so easily remain closed to the will and the grace of God? How can bigotry imbedded in your own heart be removed?

Discuss racial, social, intellectual, cultural, and other sorts of prejudice which may creep into our fellowship. How can we be more open to the Spirit of God in our congregations?

4. James was put to death while Peter was miraculously delivered. Why did God not deliver James as well as Peter? Why does God allow such things to happen? See **Isaiah 55:8–9**.

You may even now be experiencing distressing circumstances in which you question, "What is God doing?" How does Paul in **Romans 8:28** strengthen us? Name the great resource available to the Christian in the face of such mysteries (**Acts 12:5**).

With all its tremendous spiritual power, the early church did not believe its prayers had been answered; Peter's deliverance came as a shock. This is a common attitude in the church today—we pray, but we really don't believe our prayers make any difference. Prayer can easily become a meaningless spiritual exercise. Allow this study to reaffirm your conviction that prayer links you to the power of God.

Closing

Join now with your group in singing or speaking together the first stanza of "What a Friend We Have in Jesus."

What a friend we have in Jesus,
    All our sins and griefs to bear!
What a privilege to carry
    Ev'rything to God in prayer!
Oh, what peace we often forfeit;
    Oh, what needless pain we bear—
All because we do not carry
    Ev'rything to God in prayer!

To Do This Week

Read **Acts 13–15** in preparation for the next class session.

Lesson 7

The Mature Church in Labor and Hardships (Acts 13–15)

Theme Verse

" 'We must go through many hardships to enter the kingdom of God,' they said" **(Acts 14:22).**

Goal

In this lesson we will recognize and accept joyfully that, as the church under the impetus of the Holy Spirit engages in world evangelization, it must be prepared to endure great suffering and pay a great cost.

What's Going On Here?

Chapter 13 of Acts brings us to the watershed of Luke's account. In **Acts 1:8** Jesus had indicated that the spread of the Gospel would (1) begin in Jerusalem, (2) progress to all Judea and Samaria, and (3) finally reach to the ends of the earth. We have observed the realization of stages 1 and 2 in chapters 1–12 of Acts. The remainder of the book chronicles the fulfillment of the final stage—world evangelization—in the missionary journeys of Paul. It is a movement which continues today.

In the surge of the Gospel beyond the boundaries of Israel, the target of evangelism becomes more and more the Gentile population rather than the Jews. Fittingly, Luke begins in **Acts 13:9** to use the Greek name Paul rather than the Hebrew Saul when referring to this great pioneer missionary. The team of "Barnabas and Saul" **(Acts 13:2)** soon changes to "Paul and his companions" **(13:13).** From this point on, Paul remains the undisputed leader in the spread of the Gospel to the Gentile world.

As you follow the course of Paul's first journey on your Bible map, note how the work of evangelization extends gradually into a more definitely Gentile atmosphere. Paul's first recorded sermon is made in Pisidian Antioch, where there is a large Hebrew synagogue, reflecting a considerable Jewish population. When he and his companions are flung out of that city, they go 50 miles east to Iconium. Here too there is a synagogue, but it is smaller, and there are not so many Jews. Finally, upon hearing that there is a plot to take his life, Paul proceeds 40 miles to the southeast to Lystra, a town with no synagogue. Thus, we will follow the movement of the Christian faith into an entirely new atmosphere, the atmosphere of Gentile life and thought.

The official inclusion of the Gentiles into the church aroused heated argument and dissension. A certain party of Jewish Christians, the "Judaizers," sometimes called the "party of the circumcision" insisted that the Gentiles become Jewish before becoming Christian. That is, they required that Gentiles be circumcised according to the law of Moses. The circulation of this unauthorized teaching occasioned the first general church council in Jerusalem in A.D. 52. The official position of the church on the issue of circumcision was clarified there—faith alone was required for salvation. The Judaizers, nevertheless, continued to plague Paul throughout his ministry. In his letter to the churches of Galatia, the province which was the target of his first missionary journey, he clearly states the issue and gives an unequivocal answer: "We ... have put our faith in Christ Jesus that we may be justified by faith in Christ and not by observing the law" **(Galatians 2:16)**. The letter to the Galatians would provide excellent companion reading to this section of Acts.

Searching the Scriptures

1. Read **Acts 13–15.**

2. By whose initiative were Barnabas and Saul set apart for the work of missions **(Acts 13:2, 4)**? Under what conditions was the Holy Spirit able to make His will known to the church at Antioch **(vv. 1–3)**? What conditions must prevail in the church today in order that God's will may be done among us?

3. Discuss Paul's vehemence in dealing with Bar-Jesus (v. 10). Against which group did Jesus use similar forceful language? See **John 8:44.** Why was this fierceness necessary here in Acts? Whose salvation was at stake **(Acts 13:8)?** Consider this in light of Jesus' scathing denunciation in **Matthew 23:13.** For whom are the severest words in Scripture reserved?

4. Elymas was a Jewish sorcerer, or wise man. He belonged to the Jewish religion, but he trafficked in the occult. How are Christians today tempted to mix true religion with occultism? Why was blindness a fitting affliction for Bar-Jesus?

5. What was Paul's typical method upon entering a new city **(Acts 13:5, 14)?** What was the wisdom of this method?

6. Note the elements of Paul's first recorded sermon which was to a mixed Jewish/Gentile audience **(13:16–41).** How did he introduce the subject of Jesus? To what essential doctrine did he make reference in **verse 39?** What is "justification"? Use a Bible dictionary if necessary.

7. How did the listeners on this first Sabbath react to Paul's words **(v. 42)?** What incited them to speak abusively against Paul's message on the following Sabbath **(v. 45)?** What prompted their jealousy? Why is the sin of jealousy so insidious? Compare this account with **Acts 5:17** and **Matthew 27:18.**

8. What common reaction to their teaching did the missionaries experience in Iconium (**Acts 14:2**)? Why did they experience opposition (**v. 1**)? How did they respond in an unexpected manner to the opposition they encountered (**v. 3**)? What encouragement can you take from this concerning apparent failures when you share your faith in Jesus?

9. Paul performed a miracle before a totally pagan crowd in Lystra. What was the reaction of the crowd (**14:11–13**)? What should even pagans, according to the natural law in their hearts, acknowledge according to **Acts 14:17** and **Romans 1:20**? What was the "pagan sin" exemplified here? See **Romans 1:25**.

10. How is the fickleness of the human heart evidenced in **Acts 14:19**? What event from Paul's past may have come to his mind as he was being stoned?

11. Paul did not react as strongly to being stoned as he did to being worshiped. See **Acts 14:14–15**. What is the greater threat to the Christian, persecution or notoriety? Why? How did Paul and Barnabas view their sufferings (**14:22b**)? See also **2 Corinthians 4:7–12**. What had prepared Paul for these "furnace" experiences (**Acts 9:15–16**)?

12. Define the issue which threatened to divide the church in **Acts 15:1** and **5.** What contribution to the Jerusalem council was made by (a) Peter **(vv. 7–11),** (b) Paul and Barnabas **(v. 12),** and (c) James, the brother of Jesus and apparent leader of the Jerusalem church **(vv. 13–21)?**

13. What was the outcome of the dispute and whose opinion held the greatest weight **(vv. 28–29)?** How did the recommendations affect both Jews and Gentiles?

14. What caused sharp contention between Barnabas and Paul? What was the result **(Acts 13:13; 15:37–40)?**

The Word for Us

1. Read **Galatians 2** in which Paul gave his own account of the background to the Jerusalem Council. How do Paul's words shed light on Luke's comment in **Acts 15:2?** Why was this issue of such immense importance to Paul and Barnabas? What principles for dealing with similar hotly debated issues in today's church can you extract from this account in **Acts 15?**

2. What may have disillusioned John Mark and caused him to defect in **Acts 13:13?** How do Paul and Barnabas reveal their divergent natures in their reaction to John Mark's defection?

Now read **2 Timothy 4:11.** Did God give up on Mark? How did Paul's attitude later change? How did God finally use Mark mightily?

What do you do when you are tempted at times to despair of your own usefulness in God's kingdom? What lessons are there in the story of John Mark for you?

3. Old ways and prejudices do not die easily. The legalism of the Judaizers often is still present in our churches today. Many times we say, "We've never done it that way before!" All of us are strangely inclined towards trying to turn our opinions and practices into inflexible rules for everyone else to follow.

Discuss ways in which you or your congregation may be "teaching as doctrine the commandments of men" **(Matthew 15:9 RSV).**

Which things are unchangeable in the church and which things must from time to time be changed?

4. "We must go through many hardships to enter the kingdom of God" **(Acts 14:22b).** The Greek word for "hardships" here has reference to a threshing device which separates the wheat from the chaff. How does Paul's experience graphically bear out this picture of being violently tossed about and thrashed throughout his missionary life? See **2 Corinthians 11:23–28.**

Why is suffering an inevitable ingredient of kingdom work **(2 Timothy 3:12; John 15:18–20)?** In what sense are hardships not only inevitable but beneficial to those who would see God's kingdom established **(2 Corinthians 1:8–9)?** What enables the Christian to bear the cost of living for Christ **(Romans 8:17–18)?** What precisely is the cost **(Luke 14:33)?** How can you become willing to risk all in faith?

Closing

Sing or speak together this stanza of "Lord Jesus Christ, the Church's Head."

Lord Jesus Christ, the Church's head,
    You are her one foundation;
In You she trusts, before You bows,
    And waits for Your salvation.
Built on this rock secure,
    Your Church shall endure
Though all the world decay
    And all things pass away.
Oh, hear, oh, hear us, Jesus!

To Do This Week

Read **Acts 16–20** in preparation for the next class session.

Lesson 8

Nurturing Young Churches
(Acts 16–20)

Theme Verse

"Now I commit you to God and to the word of His grace, which can build you up and give you an inheritance among all those who are sanctified" (**Acts 20:32**).

Goal

In this lesson we will study the second and third missionary journeys of Paul and come to appreciate how God had instilled in him through faith great love for His church. We will also be led by God's love in Christ to serve the church as Paul did.

What's Going On Here?

In lesson 7 we traced the movements of Paul and Barnabas as they brought the Gospel of Jesus Christ to cities on the island of Cyprus and in southeast Asia Minor (modern-day Turkey). Two further journeys are chronicled in the chapters before us. The sphere of Gospel outreach becomes ever wider, extending, by the direction of the Holy Spirit, into the western regions of Macedonia and Greece, and then to west Asia Minor. We see from the westward direction of this expansion how it came about that the saving Gospel was entrusted to the Western world. With this great gift came the responsibility of delivering the Good News to those areas of the world which were as yet unevangelized. This remains the great challenge of the church.

As you study the second and third missionary journeys, the following chart along with your Bible map may help you to visualize the areas covered. Note that the Holy Spirit directed Paul to bypass west Asia Minor on the second journey, although it would have been the logical region for continuation of the work. Later, on his third journey, Paul concentrated his efforts in this bypassed area, using Ephesus as his focal point. Approximate dates of the journeys are also provided.

	Macedonia and Greece	West Asia Minor	Southeast Asia Minor	
WEST	2	3	1	EAST
	A.D. 49–51	A.D. 52–56	A.D. 46–48	

The pattern of events in each new town that Paul enters continues to be a pattern of preaching and persecution. When he is rejected by the Jews, he turns to the Greeks. When he is thrown out of one town, he proceeds to the next. We sometimes mistakenly imagine, however, that Paul rushed from place to place, meeting with success or failure, then moved on, leaving the follow-up to others. The study before us will show that this is a false impression. Having brought new churches to birth, Paul labored tirelessly to nurture them to maturity. In each successive journey he retraced the steps of his last journey for the purpose of encouraging and strengthening the churches he had founded. He remained in Corinth one and a half years and in Ephesus more than two years, pouring himself out to teach, to strengthen, and to establish the fellowship of believers there. In addition to visits, he wrote letters to these churches instructing, exhorting, consoling, and admonishing them. The legacy of these letters forms a major portion of the New Testament writings.

In this way Paul was truly carrying out Christ's commission, not only to "preach the good news to all creation" **(Mark 16:15)**, but further to "make disciples of all nations ... teaching them to obey everything I have commanded you" **(Matthew 28:19–20).** The work of evangelization includes the long-term and tedious process of nurturing. We will see that only self-sacrificing love could be the impetus for such work.

Searching the Scriptures

1. Read **Acts 16–20,** if at all possible, prior to meeting with your group.

2. As a means of acquainting yourself with Paul's second missionary journey, note the main events in these areas:

a. Derbe to Troas **(16:1–10)**

b. Philippi **(16:11–40)**

c. Thessalonica **(17:1–9)**

d. Berea **(17:10–14)**

e. Athens **(17:15–34)**

f. Corinth **(18:1–17)**

3. Discuss with your group Paul's having Timothy circumcised **(16:3)**, despite the adamant opposition which he had expressed in chapter 15 to the party of the circumcision. Consult **1 Corinthians 9:19–22** for your discussion.

4. Read **Acts 16:6–9, 14b, 18:9.** In what ways did the Holy Spirit directly involve Himself in the missionary effort? How does this demonstrate His rule in the affairs of the church?

5. Who must have joined the group in **Acts 16:10?** What probably happened to this person by **16:40?** When did he rejoin Paul **(20:5)?**

6. Compare the reception of the Gospel in the following people or groups. Match the person or group with their condition before hearing the Gospel. Discuss how this affected their reaction to the Good News.

a. Lydia **(16:14)** _____ heart, though once cold, opened to the truth through crisis

b. Philippian jailer **(16:29, 30, 33)** _____ intellectual dilettantes

c. Athenian crowd **(17:19–21, 34)** _____ fertile soil

7. What principle do you discover in **Acts 16:25** for triumphing in troubled circumstances? Remember the apostles' bodies were bruised and lacerated, and they had been thrown into a dark and deadly prison.

8. Wherein did the noble mindedness of the Bereans lie **(17:11)**? What lesson can you draw from this in regard to your own spiritual walk?

9. What special encouragement did God give Paul in Corinth **(18:9)**? Why do you think Paul needed this good word from the Lord? At what times in your life has the Lord encouraged you in a special way?

10. Review the following list of the areas covered during Paul's third journey. Note that this journey included excursions into new areas as well as return visits to formerly-evangelized cities.

a. Galatia and Phrygia: **Acts 18:23** (follow-up).

b. Ephesus and vicinity: **Acts 18:24–19:41** (new).

c. Macedonia and Greece: **Acts 20:1–6** (follow-up).

d. Return to Jerusalem: **Acts 20:7–36** (return and follow-up).

11. What is missing in the partial knowledge of the Ephesian disciples **(19:1–7)?** From whose ministry might this have resulted **(18:24–25)?** What was Paul's concern for the Ephesians in **Acts 19:2–3?** See **Romans 8:9.**

12. What do you learn from **Acts 19:13–19** about mixing sorcery with true religion? What was the effect of purging occult elements from the church in Ephesus **(19:20)?** What are you holding onto in your life which you know is contrary to God's will? How does the Holy Spirit help you to eliminate any ungodly thing from your life?

13. What did pagans typically find offensive about the Gospel and its effects on society **(19:23–27; Mark 4:16–17)?** Compare this with the main reason for Jewish opposition **(17:5).** What similar reactions to the preaching of God's Word can you identify today?

14. In **Acts 20:7–12** we find a little pattern which exhibits how the early church met. What do you learn from the passage? Of what Old Testament incidents does the miracle related in **verses 9–10** remind you?

15. What was Paul's great concern for the churches he had planted **(20:29–30)?** How was the church to counteract these dangers **(20:28, 32)?**

16. Scan **Acts 20:18–27.** On his way back to Jerusalem Paul called for the Ephesian elders to meet with him in Miletus. He reviewed with them his ministry among them and in doing so offered a portrait of a mature spiritual leader. Match the quality of a true leader with the verse in which it is mentioned or demonstrated. Some verses may depict more than one trait.

a. a humble mind   **v. 19**
b. a tender heart   **v. 22**
c. a strong will   **vv. 20, 21, 27**
d. courage to say what needs to be said   **v. 27**
e. courage to do what needs to be done   **vv. 22–24**
f. a clear objective   **v. 24**
g. a clear conscience   **v. 26**

The Word for Us

1. Look again at the account of the married couple, Aquila and Priscilla **(Acts 18:1–26).** How did God use them? See **18:2.** How does this demonstrate the truth of **1 Corinthians 12:7–11** and **Ephesians 4:16?** What is the responsibility of each member to Christ's body as a whole? How can you identify and become actively and intensely involved in the function God has given you in the church?

2. Jesus said of false teachers, "By their fruit you will recognize them" **(Matthew 7:16).** Sort out the list below into (1) characteristics of true teachers, and (2) characteristics of false teachers.

(a) Seek God's will and favor; (b) draw men to Christ; (c) want to be popular; (d) genuinely love the church and are willing to suffer for it; (e) are cool and distant; (f) manipulate; (g) serve; (h) exercise authority for the good of the body; (i) demonstrate affection; (j) use the church as a vehicle for building their ego and creating a successful career; (k) speak on their own authority; (l) base all teaching on the inerrant Word of God; (m) teach only by word, not by example; (n) exercise authority for personal profit; (o) live exemplary lives.

How can we insulate ourselves and our children against false teachers and the lure of the cults? See **Acts 20:32; Colossians 2:1–8; Acts 19:10.** When does your present involvement in Bible study become more than a virtuous exercise?

3. Paul was a persistent man. How persistent are you? What helps you stick to your goals even in the face of great odds and not give up? Perhaps the Holy Spirit is using this study to help you complete some work He has begun in you. Look up **1 Corinthians 15:58, Galatians 6:9, Ephesians 6:18, Philippians 1:27,** and **2 Timothy 1:1, 3.** In what ways does Paul ask us to be persistent? For whom are we to be persistent? Which verse(s) speaks to your heart?

4. How does your love for Jesus Christ show in your love for His church? See **1 John 5:1.** Compare your love of the church with Paul's love. Reread **Acts 20:28b** to see why Paul was willing to suffer and even die for the body of Christ.

Closing

Sing or speak together this stanza of "O Holy Spirit, Enter In."

O Holy Spirit, enter in,
    And in our hearts Your work begin,
    And make our hearts Your dwelling.
Sun of the soul, O Light divine,
    Around and in us brightly shine,
    Your strength in us upwelling.
In Your radiance
    Life from heaven
    Now is given
    Overflowing,
Gift of gifts beyond all knowing.

To Do This Week

Review your responses to the questions in "The Word for Us." Then read **Acts 21–24** in preparation for the next class session.

Lesson 9

Bound and Yet Free
(Acts 21–24)

Theme Verse

"Take courage! As you have testified about me in Jerusalem, so you must also testify in Rome" (**Acts 23:11**).

Goal

In this lesson we will see that, empowered by the Holy Spirit, the church as well as the individual Christian can move forward in God's plan despite extreme pressures and external restraints. We will also affirm that God liberated us from the bondage to sin, death, and the power of the devil through the bondage Jesus experienced as He suffered and died on the cross.

What's Going On Here?

In the foregoing lesson we tracked Paul and his companions as they carried the Good News out ever farther into the Gentile world. At the end of **Acts 20** we saw him intent on returning to Jerusalem to deliver a collection gathered from the Gentile churches. He was determined afterwards to go to Rome (**Acts 19:21**). Beginning in chapter 21, however, the great evangelist no longer moved about freely, carrying the message of salvation from one town to the next and revisiting the churches he had founded. In Jerusalem Paul was taken prisoner, and the keynote for the remainder of Acts is bondage. A wondrous fact remains: even this imprisonment was a part of God's plan. Men may be bound, but the Word of God is never bound (**2 Timothy 2:9**). Encouraged in his darkest hour by the appearance of the living Lord Himself, Paul seized every opportunity, even while imprisoned, to preach the saving Gospel.

Jesus had forewarned His followers: "You must be on your guard. You will be handed over to the local councils and flogged in the synagogues. On account of Me you will stand before governors and kings as witnesses to them" **(Mark 13:9).** Prepare to marvel as you observe how these things, point by point, are fulfilled in Paul's experience: first the local council (the Sanhedrin in Jerusalem), then the flogging, next the governors (Felix and Festus), and finally the king (Agrippa).

The particular "governor" before whom Paul stood in this session was Antonius Felix, a one-time slave who had risen in the ranks of Roman government to the position of governor of Judea. He was notorious for his base nature, cruelty, and political corruption. The Roman historian Tacitus said of him, "He held the power of a tyrant with the disposition of a slave." He lived for a time in open adultery with Drusilla, daughter of Herod Agrippa I. At age 16 she had deserted her husband for Felix and eventually became his third wife. In A.D. 59/60 Felix was called back to Rome to answer for irregularities in his governing of the Jews. This explains why he attempted to curry their favor by leaving Paul in prison, despite the apostle's obvious innocence.

Searching the Scriptures

1. Read **Acts 21–24.**

2. Review the various scenes on Paul's return journey to Jerusalem in **21:1–15.** What was the predominant tone of his meetings with believers? See especially **verses 4–6** and **12–14.**

3. What did Paul know he would encounter in Jerusalem **(20:23; 21:10–11)?** How are we to approach ministries with problems? On what basis should we enter a new ministry or leave an old one **(21:14)?** Was Paul just being stubborn or was he following God's will **(23:11)?**

4. The church leaders in Jerusalem were concerned that Paul's appearance there at Pentecost, when the city was filled with Jews from foreign lands, might incite a riot. Even Jewish Christians were not warm toward Paul. Why not **(21:20–22)?** What evidences of compromise do you detect

in the Jerusalem church? Why do you think Paul submitted to the request of these elders? Did this accommodation succeed in its intended purpose—preventing a riot (vv. 27–40)? What conclusions can you draw concerning compromise in the church?

5. Paul tried to defend himself before the Jewish mob by giving his personal testimony. Why do you think he took this risk after being beaten almost to death? What must have been his attitude toward his Jewish brothers? See **Acts 22:1, 3** and **Romans 9:3.**

6. At what point did the Jewish mob become enraged with what Paul was saying **(22:21–22)?**

7. How did Paul show in **22:23–29** that he did not glorify suffering? What might be the result of a flogging at this point? See **21:31–32.**

8. What common human fault did Paul exhibit in **23:3?** On the other hand, what very uncommon attitude did he demonstrate in **verse 5?** How do we become more submissive to God's Word as the absolute authority over our life and conduct?

9. Knowing the character and the mind-set of the Sanhedrin (**Luke 22:66** and **Acts 4:5ff.**), was it possible for Paul to receive a fair trial? What clever tactic did he use to elude their murderous intentions (**23:6–10**)?

10. **Acts 23:11** records a loving appearance of the Lord to Paul at night in prison. What must Paul's state of mind have been? Why would one commentator call this the "darkest hour" of Paul's preaching career? What was the Lord's message to him at this point? When has the Lord given you special encouragement in a time of particular need?

11. One would expect the Jerusalem church to come to Paul's defense; but that church, weakened perhaps by concession and compromise, did not come forward. What improbable sources does God use to deliver Paul (**23:10, 16**)? How does this bear out the truth of **1 Corinthians 1:25**? What special provision did God make for his servant, who was at this point beaten and weary (**23:23–24, 35**)?

12. Indicate how Paul responded to each of the charges made by Tertullus, the lawyer engaged by the Jews to present their case against the apostle before Felix in Caesarea. (See **Acts 24:5–20**.)

Tertullus' Charge	Paul's Response
He is a troublemaker who stirs up riots (**v. 5**)	**v. 12**
He is the ringleader of the Nazarene sect (**v. 5**)	**vv. 14–16**
He tried to desecrate the temple (**v. 6**).	**vv. 17–18**

What was the outcome of the trial (**v. 22**)?

13. What behavior did Paul model before the Jewish court (**23:1; 24:16**)? What is Peter's instruction (**1 Peter 3:15–16**)?

14. Describe Felix's reaction to Paul's teaching. In view of his background, character, and lifestyle, how was this reaction very understandable (**24:25**)?

15. Paul, though innocent, was to remain in prison for two years. What Old Testament character endured a similar injustice (**Genesis 40:23–41:1**)? How do the experiences of both men show that God is in control, even when His people must suffer cruel and unjust treatment?

The Word for Us

1. In **Acts 22:1–21** Paul gave a detailed account of his own religious background and his personal encounter with the Lord Jesus Christ. What stands out in his testimony?

What role does personal testimony play in sharing our faith? How is our witness of faith incomplete if we recount only our own spiritual experiences? As you have worked through Acts what have you come to understand is the focus of all who confess their faith? See **1 Corinthians 15:1–8.**

2. There is a well-known proverb which states: "He who hesitates is lost." How is this confirmed in Felix's case? Reread **Acts 24:24–26.** The fear indicated is a sincere reaction to the preaching of Paul. How can fear be a positive reaction? How might it indicate God's grace in Felix's life? What would Felix have to do in order for this grace to have effect? When did Felix find "a convenient time" to accept the Gospel message **(vv. 25–27)?** What important message in **Hebrews 3:7–8, 12–13** applies to this case? Did Paul ever give up on Felix?

3. How does your life reflect that which God has taught you through His Word? Note how very important right doctrine, right living, and right attitudes were to Paul. Why is this correspondence between one's words and one's life of such great importance? Perhaps God has shown you during this lesson something which must be changed in or removed from your life to bring it more into conformity with the teachings of His Word and the character of Christ.

4. Paul found himself in circumstances so distressing that He obviously lapsed into a depressed state which warranted the appearance of the Lord Himself. How did God help Paul? What brought peace to Paul's heart? God is still present in the lives of all believers to uphold and stabilize them no matter what the circumstances. How do you avail yourself of His nearness? What Scriptural verses do you remember which remind you of His nearness? As you refresh yourself in the sure knowledge of His presence with you, allow Him to free you from any present bondage (fears concerning health, family problems, financial straits, discouragement, worry, etc.).

Closing

Sing or speak together this stanza of "Come, Holy Ghost, God and Lord."

Come, Holy Ghost, God and Lord,
    With all Your graces now outpoured
On each believer's mind and heart;
    Your fervent love to them impart.
Lord, by the brightness of Your light
    In holy faith Your Church unite;
From ev'ry land and ev'ry tongue
    This to Your praise, O Lord, our God, be sung:
Alleluia, alleluia!

To Do This Week

Read **Acts 25–28** in preparation for the next class session.

Lesson 10

The Church Prevails
(Acts 25–28)

Theme Verse

"Boldly and without hindrance he preached the kingdom of God and taught about the Lord Jesus Christ" (**Acts 28:31**).

Goal

In this lesson we will see in the victorious experience of Paul how the Lord will always obtain His objective through the church as it moves forward in witness until the day of Christ's coming.

What's Going On Here?

We observed in the last lesson that Paul spent two years in the prison at Caesarea under the governorship of Felix. When Felix was called to Rome to give an account of his questionable handling of the Jews, he was succeeded by Festus, a man of considerable wisdom and integrity. In the chapters presently under consideration, Paul's case was brought to the attention of the new governor by Jewish officials who hoped to gain custody of the apostle with a view to killing him on the way back to Jerusalem. The result was Paul's appeal to Caesar. Before he sailed to Rome, however, Paul was given a hearing before Herod Agrippa II, king of Judea.

King Agrippa was the last of the Herods. His great grandfather had murdered the baby boys at the time of Jesus' birth. His grand uncle had ordered the execution of John the Baptist. His father, Agrippa I, had the apostle James put to death (**Acts 12:2**). Agrippa II was always described as appearing in the company of his sister Bernice. Drusilla, wife of Felix, was also a sister of this pair. At age 13 Bernice had married her uncle, Herod of Chalces. After his death she returned to her brother until she became the wife of Polemon, king of Cilicia. However, she soon abandoned him to return once again to her brother. Jewish and Roman historians report that Agrippa and Bernice were living in incest at the time of the biblical account.

In **Acts 19:21** Paul had said, "I must visit Rome also." Knowing that this strategic political and cultural center had highways which ran through all the known world, he desired to establish a base of operations for Christian service there. The Lord Himself had confirmed this direction in **Acts 23:11,** "You [Paul] must also testify in Rome." Though all the forces of men and nature seemed to combine to thwart this goal, in these final chapters Luke reported sure, slow progress until he wrote in **28:14,** "And so we came to Rome."

The book of Acts concludes with the statement that Paul though still a prisoner, continued his work to witness "boldly" and "unhindered." How it must have thrilled Luke's heart to pen that final, triumphant word "unhindered!" As Christ had foretold, the very gates of hell would not be able to prevail against His church.

The story in Acts ends somewhat abruptly. It is a fragment, not a completed history. Acts is only the first chapter in the history (*His* story) of the church, but it records what we need to know about the continuation of the work of the body of Christ. The work will go on under the headship of Christ through every decade, century, and millennium until the Lord returns.

Searching the Scriptures

1. Read **Acts 25–28.** Use a Bible map to trace the journey from Caesarea to Rome.

2. Review **25:1–12.** What plan did Jewish leaders activate as soon as Festus came into office? Did it succeed?

3. What difficulty does Festus have with Paul's case (25:13–21, 26–27)? What commendable characteristics does Festus display in these verses?

4. Paul's defense before Agrippa contains the third account of his conversion. Compare **Acts 9:1–9** (the event); **22:1–11** (Paul's testimony before the people); and **26:4–18.** What is new in this third passage?

5. Note the responses of Festus and Agrippa to Paul's testimony in **26:24, 28.** When are similar reactions voiced today against true witnesses of the Gospel? How is the burning passion of Paul's life revealed in the touching response of **verse 29?**

6. Who had really decided that Paul would sail to Italy **(Acts 23:11)?** What does the "we" of **27:1** imply?

7. Discuss Luke's graphic description of the sea voyage and the storm in chapter 27. Which details stand out for you?

8. Paul started out on the trip as one of several prisoners. By the time the voyage was over he was the hero and virtual leader of crew and passengers. What was the secret of his strength (**Acts 27:23–25**)? How is the same strength available to you in the pressures of life (**Psalm 23:4**)?

9. How is the fickleness of the human heart demonstrated in the reactions of the inhabitants of Malta to the incident of the viper (**28:3–6**)?

10. Paul remained on Malta three months. Describe his ministry there after reading **28:7–10.**

11. What did Paul do upon his arrival in Rome which typified his missionary approach in every new city (**28:17**)? What was the outcome of his efforts (**vv. 25–28**)?

12. Who remained Luke's constant center as he wrote the book of Acts? Compare **Acts 1:1** with **Acts 28:31.** What conclusions can you draw concerning the focus of the church and of the individual Christian life?

The Word for Us

1. **Psalm 107** celebrates the wondrous ways in which God delivers men from the vicissitudes of life. Read **Psalm 107:17–32.** What parallels do you find with the **Acts 27** account of the storm at sea? How did Paul carry out the injunction repeated in **Psalm 107:1, 8, 15, 21,** and **31 (Acts 27:35)?** Take time now to offer God the sacrifice of thanksgiving for His many deliverances in your life, particularly the deliverance through Christ from the bondage of sin and death.

2. Observe on your Bible map the route which eventually brought Paul from Caesarea to his God-appointed destination in Rome. Describe the nature of the route. What does this tell us about the path we may have to tread in order to reach the goals God has set for us?

3. Read again carefully Christ's words to Paul in **Acts 26:16.** Why specifically had Christ entered into Paul's experience? What was His purpose in Paul's life?

Because you, like Paul, are saved through faith in Christ, He makes your personal salvation secure! See **Romans 8:38–39.** Now, what does God want you to do with the remainder of your earthly life?

4. Paul, after his encounter with Christ on the road to Damascus, was never the same. The whole direction of his life changed; he was a man with a vision. As we study God's Word, we too encounter Christ. We should not go away unchanged. Discuss how this present lesson speaks to your life and how the entire study in Acts has affected you. In what ways do you have a stronger, clearer sense of God's plan for your life? How do you, like Paul, become equipped to ride out the storms of life until God brings you to His desired haven?

Closing

Like Paul, Jesus saved you and set you apart to testify to His love. Eagerly place yourself at God's disposal to be used wherever, whenever, and however He wants. There are still billions of people in the world who have never heard the saving Gospel. What skill or profession has God given you to make you welcome in parts of the world where missionaries cannot enter?

"Now to Him who is able to do immeasurably more than all we ask or imagine, according to His power that is at work within us, to Him be glory in the church and in Christ Jesus throughout all generations, for ever and ever! Amen" **(Ephesians 3:20–21).**

Speak or sing together this stanza of "Speak, O Lord, Your Servant Listens."

Speak, O Lord, Your servant listens,
 Let Your Word to me come near;
Newborn life and spirit give me,
 Let each promise still my fear.
Death's dread pow'r, its inward strife,
 Wars against Your Word of life;
Fill me, Lord, with love's strong fervor
 That I cling to You forever!

ACTS
The Gospel throughout the World

Leaders Notes

Preparing to Teach Acts

In preparation to teach, consult the introduction to the book of Acts in the Concordia Self-Study Bible, and if possible, read the section on Acts in the *Concordia Self-Study Commentary* (CPH, 1979).

Also read the text in a modern translation. The NIV is referred to in the lesson comments.

In the section "Searching the Scriptures" the leader guides discussion, using the questions given (or others) to help the class discover what the text actually says. This is a major part of teaching, namely, directing the learners to discover for themselves.

Another major portion of each lesson is "The Word for Us." This section helps participants, through discussion, to see the meaning of the text for our times, for church and world today, and especially for our own lives.

Group Bible Study

Group Bible study means mutual learning from one another under the guidance of a leader or facilitator. The Bible is an inexhaustible resource. No one person can discover all it has to offer. In a class many eyes see many things and can apply them to many life situations. The leader should resist the temptation to "give the answers" and so act as an "authority." This teaching approach stifles participation by individual members and can actually hamper learning. As a general rule, the teacher is not to "give interpretation" but to "develop interpreters." Of course there are times when the leader should and must share insights and information gained by his or her own deeper research. The ideal class is one in which the leader guides class members through the lesson and engages them in meaningful sharing and discussion at all points, leading them to a summary of the lesson at the close. As a general rule, don't explain what the learners can discover by themselves.

Have a chalkboard and chalk or newsprint and marking pen available to emphasize significant points of the lesson. Put your inquiries or the inquiries of participants into questions, problems, or issues. This provokes thought. Keep discussion to the point. List on the chalkboard or newsprint the answers given. Then determine the most vital points made in the discussion. Ask additional questions to fill apparent gaps.

The aim of every Bible study is to help people grow spiritually, not merely in biblical and theological knowledge, but in Christian thinking and living. This means growth in Christian attitudes, insights, and skills for Christian living. The focus of this course must be the church and the world of our day. The guiding question will be this: What does the Lord teach us for life today through the book of Acts?

Pace Your Teaching

Do not try to cover every question in each lesson. This will lead to undue haste and frustration. Be selective. Pace your teaching. Spend no more than five to 10 minutes with "Theme Verse," "Goal," and "What's Going On Here?" Take time to go into the text by topic, but not word by word. Get the sweep of meaning. Occasionally stop to help the class gain understanding of a word or concept. Allow approximately 10 to 15 minutes for "The Word for Us." Allowing approximately five minutes for "Closing" and announcements, you will notice, allows you only approximately 30 minutes for "Searching the Scriptures."

Should your group have more than a one-hour class period, you can take it more leisurely. But do not allow any lesson to drag and become tiresome. Keep it moving. Keep it alive. Keep it meaningful. Eliminate some questions and restrict yourself to those questions most meaningful to the members of the class. If most members study the text at home, they can report their findings, and the time gained can be applied to relating the lesson to life.

Good Preparation

Good preparation by the leader usually affects the pleasure and satisfaction the class will experience.

Suggestions to the Leader for Using the Study Guide

The Lesson Pattern

This set of 10 lessons is based on a significant and timely New Testament book—Acts. The material is designed to aid *Bible study*, that is, to aid a consideration of the written Word of God, with discussion and personal application growing out of the text at hand.

The typical lesson is divided into these sections:
1. Theme Verse
2. Goal
3. What's Going On Here?
4. Searching the Scriptures
5. The Word for Us
6. Closing

"Theme Verse," "Goal," and "What's Going On Here?" give the leader assistance in arousing the interest of the group in the concepts of the chapter. Here the leader stimulates minds. Do not linger too long over the introductory remarks.

"Searching the Scriptures" provides the real spade work necessary for Bible study. Here the class digs, uncovers, and discovers; it gets the facts and observes them. Comment from the leader is needed only to the extent that it helps the group understand the text. The same is true of looking up the indicated parallel passages. The questions in the study guide, arranged under subheadings and corresponding to sections within the text, are intended to help the participants discover the meaning of the text.

Having determined what the text says, the class is ready to apply the message. Having heard, read, marked, and learned the Word of God, proceed to digest it inwardly through discussion, evaluation, and application. This is done, as the study guide suggests, by taking the truths found in Acts and applying them to the world and Christianity, in general, and then to personal Christian life. Class time may not permit discussion of all questions and topics. In preparation the leader may need to select two or three and focus on them. These questions bring God's message to the individual Christian. Close the session by reviewing one important truth from the lesson.

Remember, the Word of God is sacred, but the study guide is not. The guide offers only suggestions. The leader should not hesitate to alter the guidelines or substitute others to meet his or her needs and the needs of the participants. Adapt your teaching plan to your class and your class period. Good teaching directs the learner to discover for himself or herself. For the teacher this means directing the learner, not giving the learner answers. Choose the verses that should be looked up in Scripture. What discussion questions will you ask? At what points? Write them in the margin of your study guide. Involve class members, but give them clear directions. What practical actions might you propose for the week following the lesson?

How will you best use your teaching period? Do you have 45 minutes? an hour? or an hour and a half? If time is short, what should you cut? Learn to become a wise steward of class time.

Be sure to take time to summarize the lesson, or have a class member do it. Plan brief opening and closing devotions using members of the class. Suggestions are provided in this leaders guide. In addition, remember to pray frequently for yourself and your class.

Lesson 1
The Church Is Born
(Acts 1–2)

Theme Verse
Invite a volunteer to read the theme verse for this lesson.

Goal
Read aloud the goal statement. Point out that the goal will briefly describe the direction the lesson will take.

What's Going On Here?
Read aloud or have a volunteer read aloud this introductory section.

Searching the Scriptures
1. Read aloud or summarize **Acts 1–2**. Then discuss the questions that follow.

2. **Acts 1:3** states that Jesus remained on earth to prove to His followers that He really was alive and to speak to them about the kingdom of God.

3. The two passages agree in essence. A comparison should reveal clearly that this book is a continuation of Luke's first account. In each case he highlights the occasion upon which Christ instructed His disciples to remain in Jerusalem until they received the Holy Spirit, the "gift" promised by the Father.

4. Not able to comprehend the promise of the Holy Spirit, the apostles turned the subject to something in which they had a keen interest, namely, the restoration of the kingdom of Israel. Jesus warns against speculating about the coming of the Kingdom and repeats His instruction concerning the waiting for empowerment by the Holy Spirit in order to do the work of witnesses. Ask your group how this might apply to Christians who are carried away or preoccupied with speculations concerning the date and time of Christ's return.

5. **Acts 1:8** is indeed a minioutline of Acts which unfolds exactly according to the pattern given here.

   a. The Holy Spirit is poured out on believers at Pentecost (**Acts 2**).

   b. They are empowered to be witnesses in Jerusalem (**Acts 2–7**).

   c. … in all Judea and Samaria (**Acts 8–9**).

d. ... and to the ends of the earth **(Acts 10–28)**.

This key passage gives important information concerning the nature of the church: (a) It is empowered by the Holy Spirit. (b) Its primary activity is to witness to Christ. (c) Its witness begins close at hand but expands to a universal scope.

6. Christ will return in the same manner as the believers saw Him depart. He will have the same resurrected body, and He will come in the clouds. See **Matt. 24:30** and **Rev. 1:7**.

7. He was to have accompanied Jesus during His public ministry, and he must have witnessed the resurrected Christ. Matthias is not mentioned again in Scripture, but the fact that **Acts 2:14** states, "Peter stood up with the Eleven," implies that the Holy Spirit regarded him as the twelfth apostle. Many scholars, however, argue that Paul was God's choice to fill the gap.

8. The day was Pentecost. In the Jewish calendar this was the name given to the fiftieth day after the Sabbath of Passover week. Thus, it was a Sunday. The ascension occurred on the fortieth day after the Resurrection, 10 days prior to Pentecost.

9. *An audible sign*—a sound like the blowing of a violent wind came from heaven and filled the house where the believers were assembled. *A visible sign*—"They saw what seemed to be tongues of fire that separated and came to rest on each of them" **(Acts 2:3)**.

10. It enabled them to speak in other known languages which people from various parts of the world could understand. They were not babbling, speaking what others had to interpret, or saying just anything. Instead, they had declared the wonders of God in Christ in languages they had never learned.

11. The windlike sound drew the crowds to the spot where the believers were assembled. The speaking in other tongues was obviously a way of securing the attention of the crowd. By the time Peter rose to speak, he had a captive audience.

12. Peter is addressing devout Jews, and, by linking the occurrences of Pentecost with Old Testament prophecy, he is communicating with them in their own frame of reference. The genius of this approach is demonstrated throughout Acts.

13. We are still living in these "last days," as Joel calls them. The last days are the time between the birth of Christ in Bethlehem and His Second Coming. Peter is saying that this final age is commencing with the supernatural phenomena of Pentecost.

14. Peter's boldness in proclaiming the crucified and resurrected Christ stands in glaring contrast to his cowardly denial of Jesus before a servant

girl. It is the Holy Spirit who makes the difference, the same Holy Spirit who comes to dwell in each believer at the time of salvation. Ask, "How does the Holy Spirit produce the same kind of change in you?"

15. The resurrection is the essential element of the Christian Gospel, because it sets Jesus apart from every other religious leader. None of the others (Buddah, Mohammed, the Eastern mystics, etc.) have risen from the dead. That is why it was so important that all the apostles witness to the resurrected Christ. If Jesus had not risen, His death on our behalf would have no meaning. He would be just another religious martyr or fanatic. The fact that God raised Him from the dead proves that Jesus is true God. At the same time, it is a guarantee of our own resurrection. What good news!

16. Peter directs the crowd to "repent and be baptized." To repent means to have a change of heart. In contrition the believer forsakes sin, trusting in the forgiveness of Jesus. Repentant sinners receive God's pardon by the power of the Holy Spirit.

17. These first believers devoted themselves to the apostles' teaching, which we now have written down, readily available in the Bible. They devoted themselves to fellowship, demonstrating that Christians do not live in isolation. They are members of Christ's body. They devoted themselves to the breaking of bread, the Lord's Supper, Christ's inestimable provision for strengthening His body. They devoted themselves to prayer.

18. There was unity, openness, generosity, sharing, unselfishness, love, joy in one another, hospitality, sincerity, winsomeness, and a spirit of praise. Ask the members of your group whether these attitudes characterize their personal lives as well as the corporate life of their congregation. Use such questions to stimulate self-examination, not to badger participants.

19. The Holy Spirit brought vitality to the church and its continuous growth. The key to church growth is believers who, by the power of the Holy Spirit working through God's Word, are strengthened in faith and who express boldly His love in themselves. This is infectious living; it multiplies.

The Word for Us

1. Participants should come to understand that we, as God's people, listen to His voice and, through study of the Word, come to know His will, plan, and purpose for the church as well as for the individual believer. This may mean withdrawing attention from our own plans and schemes. We pray that we focus on His will for us rather than attempting to draw His attention to things of our own design!

2. All true Christian testimony centers on Jesus Christ. The sad fact is that much so-called witnessing has nothing to do with Jesus. People may talk about going to church or about something good they have done or experienced. They may even vaguely mention God in their conversation. That is not witnessing. Jesus Christ, His purpose and work, is the center of all Christian witness. Essentially our testimony is an invitation to others to experience Jesus Christ firsthand, just as we have. See **1 John 1:1–3.**

The way we live should also point to Him; it should back up our verbal testimony. If our lifestyle contradicts what we are saying about Christ, we discredit His name and drive people away from Him. Every Christian is a witness at all times. The question is, "Am I a good one or a bad one?"

3. The verses from **1 Corinthians** and **Romans 8** tell us that each true believer has been baptized by the Holy Spirit into the body of Christ and has the Holy Spirit in him or her. God gives us His Spirit so that we may confess our sin and in faith yield ourselves to His control. This comes by the power of God at work in His Word. This will happen to an even greater extent as the Holy Spirit working through God's Word matures us in the faith. As proof of this, the fruit of the Spirit listed in **Gal. 5:22–23** will become more and more evident in our lives.

Closing

Sing or speak together the closing hymn.

To Do This Week

Urge participants to complete the suggested activities prior to the next time you meet.

Lesson 2
The Infant Church Acts
Acts 3:1–4:31

Theme Verse

Invite a volunteer to read the theme verse for this lesson.

Goal

Read aloud the goal statement.

What's Going On Here?

Read aloud or have a volunteer read aloud this introductory section.

Searching the Scriptures

1.–2. Have someone volunteer to read **Acts 3:1–10** while others pick out details. Note should be taken of the fact that Peter and John arrive at the temple at three in the afternoon during the hour of prayer following the evening sacrifice. This was a time at which many people would be assembled in the temple courts for prayer. The beggar sits at the gate called Beautiful, but he is not allowed inside because of his physical condition. Peter and John look into the eyes of this crippled man and command that he look at them. In describing the healing, Luke reveals his medical background by including details and terminology from his profession. In the original language the words for "feet" and "ankles" in verse 7, for example, are medical phrases found nowhere else in Scripture.

3. Just as with the speaking in other languages recorded in chapter 2, the Holy Spirit sets the stage here for Peter's second sermon by means of this miracle, performed in the presence of a large assembly. This confirming sign authenticates the preaching of the apostles. See **Mark 16:20.**

4. Peter gives total credit for the healing to the power of the name of Jesus. He denies any personal virtue or power in performing this miracle.

5. This question gives another good opportunity for review of truths discovered in lesson 1. Do not provide answers, but instead give participants a chance to get involved. When their list is complete, check to see that they have covered at least these points in both sermons: (a) Jesus as the center of witness; (b) the guilt of his hearers in killing Christ, the "Author of Life;" (c) the way God used their wickedness to accomplish His plan of salvation; (d) a strong witness to the resurrection (Neither Peter nor Paul ever

preached a sermon without mention of the resurrection.); (e) Jesus as the fulfillment of Old Testament prophecy concerning the Christ; (f) the call to repentance.

6. Throughout the Old Testament, such prophets as Moses, Samuel, and Isaiah prophesied of Christ. He was to come through the Jewish nation. The salvation He won was to be offered first to the Jews. Jesus had indicated that witness concerning Him would begin in Jerusalem and would radiate from there throughout the earth.

7. The priests and captain of the temple guard had probably been summoned by the Sadducees who were outraged by the teaching of the resurrection of Christ. This is because they denied the supernatural and refused to accept the reality of life after death.

8. (a) Peter and John were seized and imprisoned. (b) The church grew to about 5,000 people.

9. Ask the group to think of a present-day investigating team of comparable prominence and power (e.g., the FBI, an internal audit committee, a church board). The point is that this was a highly intimidating group, supposedly the men with the power in the Jewish world. The apostles were up against staggering odds, humanly speaking.

10. The Holy Spirit, together with the actual presence of Christ within these men, tipped the scales in their favor, not any personal strength or merit. Don't neglect to read the very powerful and encouraging passage from **Luke 12** with your group. It is the Holy Spirit in our lives who enables us to do everyday tasks as well as to prevail against impossible odds.

11. It is important that, in examining this passage, participants understand that Peter and John do not espouse some personal cause such as freedom of speech or equal rights. What they do and say is accomplished in God's power for God's purposes. The risk is taken, the boldness is generated so that testimony to the death and resurrection of Christ might be given. God uses hardships and opposition as opportunities for Christians to testify to the power of God's love in Christ in their lives. Allow time for participants to give examples.

12. In absolute rebellion against God's truth, these religious leaders stand opposed to the Gospel in the face of irrefutable evidence. People today sometimes say that they would believe if God showed them a miracle. That is not true. This group had seen a miracle and still refused to believe. Unbelief comes not from lack of facts, but from the natural condition of the heart which is desperately wicked.

13. The disciples do not retaliate in self-righteousness, self-defense, or arrogance. They humbly submit to the will and demands of a living God.

14. The first strategy of the church is to pray, turning the whole matter over to the all-wise and sovereign God who has created them. They do not ask that the persecution cease; rather they ask that the work of Christ's church might continue. They ask that they might be able to go on speaking boldly in His name and to continue performing signs which would draw the lost world to Him. God supplied them the boldness to confess their faith in Jesus.

15. The building where the believers were assembled quaked. Note that there was not a repetition of speaking in tongues, but that the central work of the Holy Spirit through believers did occur, testifying to Christ. Another evidence of the presence of the Holy Spirit among these believers was the love, unity, and selflessness which they spontaneously expressed toward one another.

The Word for Us

1. That the healing performed by Peter and John in **Acts 3** is similar to the healings of Jesus in **Mark 2** and **John 5** beautifully testifies to the truth that the church, the body of Christ, continues the activity of Christ. In these apostles, Jesus was still at work doing exactly what He had done in His days on earth. Like Christ, the church is to make personal, immediate, direct contact with suffering people. In Jesus' name the church offers to a lame humanity not just alms to help it maintain life, but something to cure the affliction itself—healing through the blood of Jesus shed on the cross.

There is much talk about miraculous signs in present-day Christianity. One could get the impression that if these happenings are not present in our church experience, our spiritual life is below par; we are not "Spirit-filled."

God surely can and does still heal. He does so in accordance with His boundless mercy and His sovereign will. He does so in response to the prayer of faith. See **James 5:15.** But God does not always heal, and He certainly is not obligated to heal upon command. The healing miracles recorded in Acts were necessary as a means of authenticating Christ's followers. See **Mark 16:20.** The Word confirms our preaching and teaching today.

The danger in seeking after signs is that we make these, rather than Christ, the focus of our faith and of our spiritual experience. The desire for the sensational, as Jesus indicated, is a fleshly desire. Remember, real evidences of being Spirit-filled are love, unity, infectious joy, and a bold witness to Christ.

2. In denying the existence of angels, the immortal spirit of man, and the resurrection, the Sadducees rejected a literal interpretation of Scripture, and they denied the power of God to raise Jesus from the dead. Although

they could not refute the fact that a notable miracle had been accomplished, they refused to acknowledge God's hand in this. These men, then, were none other than the rationalists of their time. It is important to see that the great enemies of the preaching of the Gospel are not the sinners; the great antagonism comes from the religious leaders who deny the Word of God either by their lips or by their lives.

3. The name of Jesus carries with it the character and the authority of Jesus. God promises to hear us because of the completed work of redemption by His Son. Thus when we pray "in the name of Jesus," we are telling the heavenly Father that we trust Him to hear us for Jesus' sake and that our purpose is to glorify Him and see His work accomplished through us on earth. We are saying that we believe our petition is consistent with His will for us in Jesus Christ, our Lord.

The church is the body of Christ on earth and so functions in His authority. The power that He has is limitless, and it is on the basis of that power that He sends His followers into the world. "All authority ... has been given to Me. *Therefore* go ..." **(Matt. 28:18–19).** If we, the church, seem to have lost power, perhaps we are not functioning "in the name of Jesus." This would mean we have exchanged His will and purpose for our own plans and schemes.

4. Often we feel that God has no use for us in spiritual matters because of our inadequacies, inexperience, or lack of training. The account of Peter and John as unschooled and undistinguished men lays those excuses to rest. Take another look at **Luke 12:11–12** and encourage participants with these verses. See also the marvelous promise in **2 Cor. 9:8.**

Closing

Sing or speak together the closing hymn.

To Do This Week

Urge participants to complete the suggested activities prior to the next class session.

Lesson 3
Growing Pains
Acts 4:32–5:42

Theme Verse
Invite a volunteer to read the theme verse for this lesson.

Goal
Read aloud the goal statement.

What's Going On Here?
Read aloud or have a volunteer read aloud this introductory section.

Searching the Scriptures
1.–2. The church was overflowing with love which led to giving up personal possessions to meet the needs of the body. Bold witness, the church's central work, persisted.

3. It is important for the group to discover that Ananias and Sapphira did not sin in holding back part of their profit. There was no legislation for giving; they were not required to give all or even part of their earnings. They wanted to appear to have given all, perhaps so that they might seem to be as devout as Barnabas. This is the sin of hypocrisy. It was flagrant and premeditated, an affront to the sovereignty of God.

It was Satan who suggested to the couple that they might lie to God. He is the "father of lies" **(John 8:44)** and his chief method is deception **(Rev. 12:9)**. However, it was by their own will that Ananias and Sapphira acted upon the suggestion.

Ask participants if we are ever justified in saying, "The devil made me do it." Read **1 Cor. 10:13** for a very encouraging promise concerning the Christian's ability to resist temptation. Satan may oppress the Christian, but he can never possess the Christian. See **John 10:29.**

4. Sin, like cancer, must be removed to prevent its spread. This act of severe judgment on the sin of hypocrisy in the church sets a standard. We should take it as a solemn warning in our own church life.

5. The swift discipline was followed by a sense of tremendous awe. The "fear" which gripped the church was a fitting recognition of the reality and majesty of God, something which Ananias and Sapphira had not acknowledged. "Be not deceived, God is not mocked" **(Gal. 6:7 KJV).**

6. *Ekklesia* is the Greek word for "church." It was used in Greek political and social life to mean "an assembly." Its literal meaning is "that which is called out." The church is God's people who are called out of the world and separated to exist for Him.

7. Many miraculous healings followed the severe judgment upon the sin of hypocrisy. Note that all were healed; there were no failures. No one was sent unhealed, "because they did not have faith." In order to measure up, modern-day faith healers would have to be able to heal people by their mere shadow crossing the sick bed, and they would be allowed no failures.

The purpose of church discipline is to call sinners to repent and to trust the forgiveness of Christ Jesus. Cleansed through faith in Jesus, Christians become an instrument of God's healing to the world.

8. The growth and activity aroused extreme jealousy among the Sadducees. Remember this sect did not believe in the supernatural, yet healings were happening all around. The leaders had the apostles imprisoned and were, no doubt, considering how to eliminate them.

9. The Word of God cannot be bound. The apostles were miraculously released by an angel for the purpose of returning to the temple to preach. Their response was one of total submission.

It is clear from the rest of Acts and of church history that God does not intend always to get His people physically out of prison, but it is also clear that "where the Spirit of the Lord is, there is freedom" **(2 Cor. 3:17).**

10. The gathering of the whole Sanhedrin was rare and no doubt presented a very imposing scene. These were the richest, most influential, and most powerful men in the Hebrew culture. They undoubtedly came in full array with great pomp and circumstance. Imagine their consternation when this august assembly received the message that the prisoners were not to be found. It must have caused a terrific double take. Imagine their further embarrassment when these leaders learned that the apostles were right back in the temple teaching the people.

11. The high priest testifies to the far-reaching influence of the Christian movement. He indicates that the teaching of the apostles is turning public opinion to a true understanding of the Crucifixion—the Jews are guilty of the blood of their own longed-for Messiah!

12. Again the sermon contains the fundamental truths of the Gospel—the death, resurrection, and ascension of Christ and the call to repentance. Peter never waters down his testimony but always confronts his listener with the claims of Christ. At this point he does so in direct defiance of the Hebrew court and in confirmation of his bold claim, "We must obey God rather than men." The Holy Spirit is his partner in witness.

13. The Holy Spirit is given to those who receive Christ as Savior and

then walk under His Lordship. We are, of course, to obey those in authority. Only in cases where the demands of our rulers are clearly in conflict with the Word and will of God are we justified in refusing to submit.

The Greek word for "obey" here is a very rare one. It means actual, absolute, unquestioning obedience. We are to give God such obedience, and we can joyfully do so because He is utterly trustworthy.

14. Words such as reasonable, distinguished, cautious, cool-headed, sage would characterize Gamaliel. He advises that the apostles be left alone. If the work is not of God, it will die out on its own; if it is of God, fighting against it will be to no avail.

This is good advice. Ask participants to examine their own lives to see if there are areas in which they are fighting against God. Applying Gamaliel's advice can bring release and peace.

15. Jesus had predicted that precisely the suffering endured by the apostles on this occasion (interrogation by high officials and flogging) was inevitable. He also promised that such trials would be a cause for rejoicing. They linked the sufferer with the prophets of old and with Jesus Himself. Persecutions and suffering were signs that authentic service to Christ was occurring.

16. Holding to Christ above all else no matter what the cost, a warm and loving inner life, and persistence in the work of witnessing continue to characterize the church.

The Word for Us

1. Throughout Scripture when God initiates a new order among His people we find Him dealing with sin by an act of swift judgment. In doing so He sets a standard of purity, absolute honesty, and submission to His sovereign Lordship. We must not think that, because there is so little evidence of such holiness in the church as we see it, we can ignore God's call to purity. It is still God's will and design for His church. Above all we should search our own hearts to see if dishonesty or hypocrisy in any form lurks there. We must, as Christians, be absolutely honest in all our dealings (taxes, investments, purchases, etc.) even if this is to our personal disadvantage. Furthermore, we must guard against hypocrisy. Do we really mean what we profess and sing publicly in our worship services? We may sing most heartily, "Take my life, O Lord, renew" and then go out to live lives which are completely self-centered and self-directed. This is hypocrisy.

Note: It was God who passed judgment on the sin of Ananias and Sapphira. There was probably no one more surprised than Peter when Ananias fell dead at his feet.

2. Read through these soul-searching questions. As participants ponder them, have one member read **Psalm 15** which holds before us God's high standard of holiness. Note how the conditions of holiness delineated in this psalm correspond to the details of the Ananias/Sapphira episode.

Knowing that we too fall short of this standard, we can find forgiveness and the sure comfort of God as we confess our failings to Him. Use **Ps. 51:1–17** as a prayer of contrition. As someone reads these verses aloud, have the other participants bow in silent prayer.

3. Deal with this question simply by reading the verses in **1 Peter.** They can minister real peace to those who are currently passing through deep waters. The topic of suffering for Christ will come up again in the next lesson and throughout Acts, so you will not need to dwell on it at this point.

4. In **John 15:26–27** Jesus referred to two witnesses—the Holy Spirit and the Christian. It should help us to realize that, while witnessing is an awesome responsibility, we are not alone in it. As we faithfully deliver the Gospel message, the Holy Spirit conveys the power of its truth. Unbelievers may laugh and scoff at the testimony, but the Holy Spirit keeps calling them to hear and obey God's Word. The Holy Spirit working through God's Word strengthens our faith to enable, to empower, and to motivate us to confess boldly our faith in Christ Jesus.

Closing

Sing or speak together the closing hymn.

To Do This Week

Urge participants to complete the suggested activities prior to the next session.

Lesson 4
Marks of Maturity
Acts 6–7

Theme Verse

Invite a volunteer to read the theme verse for this lesson.

Goal

Read aloud the goal statement.

What's Going On Here?

Read aloud or have a volunteer read aloud the introductory section.

Searching the Scriptures

1.–2. Participants should note that there were no ethnic differences here. All the disputants were Jewish. Only their culture, language, and attitudes differed. This subtle sort of prejudice probably exists in every local church. What prejudices lurk in our own hearts? Which people do we ignore because they differ from us in social, intellectual, or ethnic background?

3. The ministry of the Word of God and of prayer is distinguished from the business aspects of church life. What's the lesson here for our local churches? The pastor needs time for the study of God's Word and prayer.

He should not be expected to be an organizer, a promoter, a sort of vice-president, or a manager.

Although preaching the Word is the primary work of the church, the support work, the waiting on tables, is not presented as inferior. It too is a high and holy work. This is made clear by the spiritual qualifications of the seven—spirituality, wisdom, and prayer.

4. Rather than ignoring the problem as too trivial, the apostles deal with the disturbance immediately. They act maturely by nipping the problem in the bud, look at it calmly rather than fly into a rage, and resolve it with God's help. The result of this was further rapid growth in the church.

5. The seven were chosen by the church and ordained by the apostles. This gives some insight into the workings of the church. The whole body was involved in this major decision, but final authority rested with the apostles.

6. As a solution to the problem, the church chose seven Hellenists—

men from the very company of those who thought their widows were neglected. It is in the spirit of Christianity to overcome prejudice by giving to those who think they have been treated unjustly the honors and responsibilities to help resolve the situation.

Ask the group whether this example suggests a fresh approach to similar antagonisms they may encounter.

7. Stephen, though a layman, was noted for his faith, his spiritual power, and his wisdom. In chapter 7 we will observe his courage and love. His articulate defense before the Sanhedrin shows that his heart was filled with the Word of God. Call attention to the fact that Stephen does not confine his ministry to the business of the church. He is out in the world, willing to die for the Gospel.

8. Through the laying on of hands Stephen is associated with the apostles, and their ministry is extended to him along with the other six men. This is something new in the church and, characteristically, it is confirmed by the accompanying signs and wonders.

9. The members of the Synagog of the Freedmen consisted of persons who had been freed from slavery. They came from different Hellenistic areas. They were unable to refute Stephen, because of the wisdom of the Holy Spirit, who resided in him. This is a marvelous fulfillment of Jesus' promise in **Luke 21:15.** Ask the group to look it up. It is a promise made to us as well as to Stephen.

10. Stephen is accused of blasphemy against Moses (the Law), God, and the temple. The same charge concerning the destruction of the temple was leveled against Jesus. Jesus too was accused of blasphemy because He made Himself equal with God.

The charges against Stephen are particularly insidious, because they contain half-truths. The temple would be destroyed, yet without loss, for God would dwell in human hearts, by grace, not by law.

11. The consternation and agitation of this austere assembly stands in striking contrast to the serene and angelic radiance of Stephen's face. He is obviously the one in control. Do not fail to have participants look up the beautiful supporting text from **2 Corinthians.**

12. This question covers 50 verses in **Acts 7.** Do not attempt to read the whole passage during the session. Instead, become familiar with it beforehand so that you can help participants discover these truths in Stephen's speech:

a. *God's method.* He shows the persistent working of God throughout Israel's history. Note how many times Stephen refers to God in the account. Point out verses like **7:9–10, 17, 35, 44.**

b. *Man's hindrance.* He highlights the repeated rebellion of the Jews and their attempt to thwart God's purposes. Draw attention to the theme of rejection in **verses 9, 35, 39.**

    c. *God's victory.* God continually advances and fulfills His promise in the person of the Righteous One, despite the hindrances of men. See **verses 9–10, 35, 44.**

    13. Stephen is no longer defendant but accuser. With total disregard for his own safety, he lashes out against the stiff-necked people who even now are intent upon opposing God's revelation through Stephen himself. His mangled body is evidence of Jerusalem's refusal to yield to the Spirit. This confirms Jesus' mournful observation concerning the city in **Luke 13:34.**

    14. Stephen's listeners were physically circumcised. But they were uncircumcised in their hearts and ears. The external ritual of circumcision was to signify an internal change, a covenant with God according to His promise. But God's Word had no entrance through uncircumcised ears and so made no difference inwardly, in their hearts. Note that in **verse 57** they cover their ears, stubbornly rejecting God's message. Their external ritual had become a sham.

    It can often be said of us today: "These people honor Me with their lips, but their heart is far from Me" **(Matt. 15:8).** Present this thought to participants as a stimulus for discussion.

    15. Like Christ, Stephen enters death with confidence. "Father, into Thy hands I commend My Spirit." Stephen heroically forgives his murderers. He falls asleep in peace. These similarities are evidence of Stephen's vibrant faith in Christ. Jesus lived in Stephen. He lives in us. Maturity means to conform to the image of Christ. **Phil. 3:10** corresponds beautifully with this scene.

    16. Stephen attested to the reality of angels and of heaven. He challenged the Sadducean theory that the supernatural does not exist. Stephen saw the unseen.

    17. Saul is introduced here as an outright enemy of the church.

The Word for Us

    1. The office of the seven was introduced into the church in response to a need. There is little detail given, no evidence of a fixed pattern. The primary force in the work of Christ's church is the sure guidance of the Holy Spirit.

    The importance of all jobs in the church is underscored by the fact that those in charge of its business and service aspects were also to have spiritual qualifications. Consider Stephen as a prime example. He was not involved only in the business aspects of the church. Stephen was firmly grounded in the Word. He carried it out into the marketplace. That is the job of all Christians.

2. The more we study Stephen's character, testimony, suffering, and final triumph, the better we understand his dependence on Christ in each of these areas. As the group meditates on Stephen's character, pray that the Holy Spirit will lead you to discover for yourselves the secret of spiritual maturity—abiding in Christ. Remind participants that God has provided us the means—His Word—by which we can grow in faith to spiritual maturity.

3. A very dynamic young church nurtured Stephen to full stature. These first Christians had no buildings, programs, committees, or boards, but they had one another and they ministered their gifts to one another. Maturity depends on vital participation in the Word and Sacrament ministry of the body.

The church today can provide the same nurturing environment. When believers actively and intensely involve themselves in the means God has given them, the whole body of Christ grows. One of the aims of this Bible study is to cause participants to identify and use their spiritual gifts so that the body becomes better equipped for service.

4. Read through the questions together and discuss how people resist Christian witness today with criticism, disfavor, and disdain for the message. Ask if someone can share a time when God gave special grace to meet these difficulties. Others may be able to cite examples of dying grace which God has granted to believers they have known.

Closing

Sing or speak together the closing hymn.

To Do This Week

Urge participants to complete the suggested activities prior to the next class session.

Lesson 5

Thrust Out of the Nest

Acts 8–9

Theme Verse

Invite a volunteer to read the theme verse for this lesson

Goal

Read aloud the goal statement.

What's Going On Here?

Read aloud or have a volunteer read aloud this introductory section.

Searching the Scriptures

1. Participants will benefit most from this study if they have read through the Scripture portions carefully. This preparation will result in rich, deep, Bible-based discussion.

2. Persecution precipitated the scattering of believers which resulted in the spread of the Gospel outside Jerusalem. External attack has never been a real threat to the ongoing life of the church. On the contrary, it has strengthened it and caused it to multiply. One Bible scholar suggests that persecution is the missing ingredient in the life of the church in North America today. You may wish to put this suggestion before your group for discussion. Perhaps Christians are not persecuted because they have not confronted the world, but have made compromises with it. Discuss other reasons why Christians may be ridiculed today.

3. Do look up the familiar parable in Matthew. Note that the "good seed" are the "children of the kingdom." Discuss what should characterize our lives if we, like Stephen and Philip, are to be good seed in the world.

4. Be sure your group is aware that this is not Philip, the apostle, but Philip, the evangelist, one of the seven chosen along with Stephen to "wait on tables." He too shared the Gospel, and the authenticity of his witnessing of faith was confirmed by signs and wonders.

5. This is a sticky passage. Let us rely upon the Holy Spirit to give us light, and to resist the temptation to go beyond the information in the text in order to come up with a pat answer. In **verse 13** Luke indicates that Simon believed and was baptized. This would imply a genuine faith. Yet Peter states in **verse 21** that Simon's heart was not right before God.

Simon may have given intellectual assent to Philip's preaching and entered into the external ritual of Baptism, but there was no real change of heart, no conversion, or he may have given in to temptation and fallen from faith. Reserve detailed discussion of this point for "The Word for Us." Simony is the commercial selling of something sacred.

6. This again is a difficult passage. For the present, simply observe the facts as stated in the text. The issue of receiving the Holy Spirit will be treated under "The Word for Us."

7. The Ethiopian's attention was already arrested by the written Word. His heart was searching for the truth of the Gospel. The Holy Spirit had prepared this field as well as the instrument (Philip) for planting the seed in it. This remarkable account shows how God is directly in charge of the forward movement of His church.

8. Devise some way to work through these longer passages in a limited period of time. This will be easier if each participant has read the assigned chapters prior to the class session. The story of Saul's conversion is a familiar one and could perhaps be effectively covered by having members recount the events of the story in a chain narration—each participant supplies one detail from the story in sequence. This is an open-Bible exercise.

9. Here we have the great truth that Christ and His church are one. It ought to be a wonderful encouragement to note that Jesus identifies with His church. It is not just an organization which He set into motion and then left to its own devices. It is His extension of Himself on earth, His body. He is the head, the captain, the acting director, and He ever watches over the workings of His church. To persecute the church is to persecute Jesus.

10. Ananias is referred to simply as a "disciple," i.e., an ordinary believer. God appoints ordinary people for extraordinary tasks, so that His power and sovereignty might be revealed through them. Share this revealing definition of "God's giants" with your group: God's giants are little people who undertake great things with God's strength.

11. Saul immediately began preaching Jesus as the Son of God. This stands in contrast to Simon's questionable conversion. When the Spirit of Christ regenerates our hearts, we bear witness to Christ.

12. The "many days" of **Acts 9:23** was a period of three years, the major part of which was probably spent in Arabia. This speaks in favor of spiritual retreat—a time spent in conference with Christ, a time of reconstruction, a time of waiting upon the Lord in preparation for the work He has for us.

13. The healthy church is here characterized by rest, edification, fear of the Lord, comfort of the Holy Spirit, and growth.

14. The healing of Aeneas and the raising of Dorcas bear many parallels

to Jesus' healing of the paralytic **(Luke 5:18–26)** and the raising of Jairus' daughter **(Mark 5:37–43)**. Peter's instructions to Aeneas **(v. 34)** and to Tabitha, or Dorcas, **(v. 40)** echo the very words that Jesus used. The church does indeed carry on "all that Jesus began to do and to teach" **(Acts 1:1)**.

15. Dorcas illustrates the gift of "helps" or service in the church. Christians who, out of love for the poor and needy, make garments for the poor or perform a similar task, render an important service to the Lord.

The Word for Us

1. Every believer receives the gift of the Holy Spirit upon conversion. The signs which often accompanied that infilling were not granted the Samaritans until the apostles laid hands on them. This established once and for all that the church is a unity. The receiving of the Spirit was a sign to Jewish Christians that these Samaritans were members of the body of Christ just as certainly as Jewish believers were. The use of the apostles as instruments for this infilling was a sign to the Samaritans that they were not to start their own brand of Christianity distinct from the Jews.

Historically, that is exactly what the Samaritans had done with the Jewish religion; they had adopted Jewish teaching but had developed a separate form of Judaism. God is saying by this act, "There are not two bodies but only one. There is one church and the Samaritans belong to it equally with the Jews."

2. As a persecutor of the church and an ardent Pharisee, Saul's personality is clearly aggressive, zealous, vehement, relentless, even ruthless. These traits, when out of control, are negative and destructive. Note, however, that these same qualities, when surrendered to the control of Christ, are positive and useful. The fierce persecutor of the church became fiercely devoted to the preaching of the Gospel. His vehemence and persistence became valuable assets in mission work. In **Acts 9:5** Saul addresses Jesus as "Lord." That is the key to the transformation of his basic personality into something of use in the Lord's work.

We may see that this is true of Saul but fail to admit the application to our own lives. We regard ourselves as too timid and weak, too headstrong, too tainted by sinful inclinations to qualify for useful work in God's kingdom. However, the Spirit of God calls each of us to surrender our lives afresh to His service. He has the power to bring about the necessary transformation of our character. See **2 Cor. 5:17.**

3. Simon, a magician, sought the external signs of Christianity, the wonders and the miracles. It is as if he wanted to add these to his bag of occult practices. He was not seeking God, only the things of God.

The Ethiopian, on the other hand, was a proselyte to Judaism, which indicates that he was seeking the true God. He had been to the feast in Jerusalem where he had obtained a copy of the ancient book of Isaiah. He was hungry for God. When Philip came to offer the Bread of Life, the Ethiopian was ready to receive it.

4. Remind your group that at some time all Christians may be weak and need help or encouragement. The list of qualifications should be applied to that area of our lives as well. There are people in our midst who are spiritually starved: lonely, elderly people with only the television for a companion; professional people driven by the craving for recognition; husbands and wives who find their love dwindling; young people drifting into dependence on alcohol, drugs, and sex; even professional church workers who, in frustration, have lapsed into a meaningless routine. Remind participants that the Holy Spirit working through the Word of God strengthens the faith of believers equipping them to be used for winning souls. When we fail to use the gifts God has provided, we approach Him confidently and humbly asking for forgiveness. Through faith in Jesus we receive complete forgiveness and the power to serve Him faithfully.

Closing

Sing or speak together the closing hymn.

To Do This Week

Urge participants to complete the suggested activity prior to the next time the class meets.

Lesson 6

Broadening Horizons

Acts 10–12

Theme Verse

Invite a volunteer to read the theme verse for this lesson.

Goal

Read aloud the goal statement.

What's Going On Here?

Read aloud or have a volunteer read aloud this introductory section.

Searching the Scriptures

1. You may wish to read chapters 10 and 11 here and chapter 12 after question 9.

2. The character of Cornelius was quite remarkable. In contrast to the idol-worshiping world from which he came and which surrounded him, he had become a man of faith in the one God. Although a military person of discipline and toughness, he expressed this faith through devotion, almsgiving, and prayers. His godliness obviously influenced his whole household.

3. Like the Ethiopian, Cornelius was eager to know God. However, he still needed God's full deliverance from sin.

God sees an honest heart which truly seeks Him. Cornelius was not yet saved; he needed the power of the Gospel. God would see to it that Cornelius got it just as the Ethiopian did.

4. The Lord is teaching Peter that he is no longer under the ceremonial laws of the Old Covenant in which there was a distinction between clean and unclean foods. The threefold repetition made this new teaching especially emphatic, because the practices of Judaism were so deeply entrenched in Peter's life and thinking.

Not until Peter hears Cornelius' account does he come to a full understanding of God's teaching in this vision, namely, that not only certain foods but Gentiles are no longer to be regarded as unclean.

5. God was moving independently of human volition. Peter rather disdainfully explained that he would never have come to Cornelius' house without God's insistence. By inviting the Gentile visitors to lodge with him in Joppa, Peter showed that the light was beginning to break upon his thinking.

6. Note that Peter's message on this occasion contains no quotations from the Old Testament. A Gentile audience would not be familiar with these. The essential Gospel remains the same: the life, death, and resurrection of Jesus Christ, and the forgiveness of sins offered in Him. This will be covered more fully in a later discussion.

7. The outpouring of the Holy Spirit with the evidence of speaking in tongues was the conclusive proof that these Gentiles were accepted into fellowship on the same basis as the Jews. Speaking in tongues did not always accompany the outpouring of the Spirit, but here it demonstrated that in Christianity Jews and Gentiles were equal.

8. The church at Antioch came into being as a result of the scattering

after Stephen's death. Believers there first witnessed exclusively to the Jews but eventually extended the Gospel also to the Greeks (Gentiles). God's hand of blessing was in this effort and a strong local church emerged. Barnabas was sent by the Jerusalem church to investigate and found evidence of the grace of God—a new tone and disposition of joy, light, and happiness all of which characterize the presence of the Spirit.

9. Essential elements of church life present in Antioch included: (1) the exercise of spiritual gifts, e.g., the prophecy of Agabus; (2) devotion to Christ; (3) teaching from Scripture by strong leaders; (4) proclamation of the Gospel; (5) concern for the body as expressed in mutual sharing and meeting of needs.

10. James was the first of the 12 apostles to be martyred. Believers undoubtedly thought God would protect these leaders, and this was a crushing blow. It drove the church to its knees. Though not always so composed, Peter was obviously helped by the prayers of the church and so slept between his guards the night before his scheduled execution.

11. The Hebrews passage teaches that angels are appointed to minister to God's people. They guide, protect, and strengthen. They even ministered to Jesus in **Matt. 4:11.**

12. How often are we surprised when our prayers are answered? Or, worse, do we attribute the answers to chance, coincidence, or good luck? God instructs us to pray without doubting. Jesus clearly showed that prayer has real power. He prayed frequently. Note that God graciously responded even to these doubting prayers.

13. In the stubborn rebellion of his heart Herod refused to acknowledge Peter's deliverance as a divine act. This is the sin of the pagan—he shuns the light God gives him. This defiance of God reaches its peak when Herod receives praise which belongs only to God.

14. Herod is dead. The Word of God is alive, and the chapter ends with Barnabas, Paul, and Mark going down the highway to carry this living Word into all the world. God is sovereign; His purposes prevail.

The Word for Us

1. How fortunate we are to have the account of Cornelius. He became a worshipper of the true and living God. In **Rom. 1:18–20** Paul describes the more common pagan reaction to the evidence of God in creation. Instead of worshiping God, people generally worshiped the creature more than the Creator and made idols for themselves. All who do not put their trust in the Triune God for salvation through Christ Jesus remain under God's judgment and are eternally dead in trespasses and sins. In the story of Cornelius we have the assurance that God seeks and saves those who are lost.

2. It would have been inappropriate for Peter to include references to the Old Testament in this message to a Gentile audience. The essentials of the Gospel remain constant, and they are sufficient though the Holy Spirit works to bring conversion. Those present received the message of Christ and were baptized. Peter had more to say, but it was not necessary. The Holy Spirit interrupted him. He is the one who brings people to repentance using human messengers as instruments who share God's Word about Jesus.

3. Pray privately for the Holy Spirit to guide this discussion and change hearts where necessary. He alone can bring about right thinking, unity, and Christlikeness in our churches.

We open ourselves to the leading of the Spirit as we study His Word and act in obedience to what we discover there.

We also must make ourselves available to God by presenting ourselves to Him daily **(Rom. 12:1–2)**, reading and studying His Word, communing with Him in prayer, and following His commands.

4. God did not deliver James from disaster but immediately afterwards delivered Peter. This reveals that He could have delivered James; He had the power to do so. God is not hindered by any circumstance. There is infinite comfort in that, because we know that, even though James was taken, God was in control. He who could deliver Peter and, in wisdom, did so, was equally wise when He did not deliver James from the hands of enemies. Through faith in Jesus God did deliver this life of burden into glorious eternal life with Him in heaven. Life cannot be fully understood in the process of living it; we must wait. Meanwhile, we come to rest in the infinite wisdom of God's loving control.

We are still in the midst of such mysteries. People are taken from us, often through pain, whom God mightily used and without whom we thought we could not live. We rest assured in God's promise of eternal life. Prayer remains the same great resource it was in the early church.

Closing

Sing or speak together the closing hymn.

To Do This Week

Urge participants to complete the suggested activity prior to the next time the class meets.

Lesson 7

The Mature Church in Labor and Hardships
Acts 13–15

Theme Verse

Invite a volunteer to read the theme verse for this lesson.

Goal

Read aloud the goal statement.

What's Going On Here?

Read aloud or have a volunteer read aloud this introductory section.

Searching the Scriptures

1.–2. The important principle to be discovered here is that the Holy Spirit is the moving force in the whole missionary endeavor. The call to the full-time ministry must come from Him. The church cooperates by waiting upon Him with prayer, worship, and fasting and then by obeying when He makes His will known. God still works in His church today.

3. Paul was gentle, patient, and understanding, but where Satan was at work to hinder the turning to truth of a lost soul, Paul reacted fiercely. Jesus did the same. His vehemence was directed, not only against prostitutes and sinners, but also against false religious teachers who stood between men and God.

4. Many who call themselves Christians also are willing to become involved with astrology, tarot-card reading, superstitious charms, and other forms of occultism. Such practices have no place in the life of a Christian. To be a Christian means to be living in relationship with the Lord Jesus Christ. That pure relationship excludes even the slightest hint of occultism, which is Satan's realm.

Elymas' temporary blindness was a reflection of his spiritual darkness. He, like the Jewish nation, rejected the light of the Gospel and tried to stand in the way of the salvation of the Gentile Sergius Paulus.

5. Paul probably worshiped on Sunday together with other Christians either in a private dwelling or in some prearranged place of meeting. But whenever he entered a new city where there was a synagog, he took the opportunity to be there on the Sabbath. It was the custom in these synagogs to invite visitors from the Jewish homeland to speak. This afforded

Paul a wonderful opportunity to preach the Gospel to a ready-made crowd.

6. Paul rehearses Jewish history to show that Jesus is the fulfillment of Old Testament prophecy. The life, death, and resurrection of Jesus remains the central Gospel message. The word *justification* is introduced here for the first time in Acts. It is a favorite term of Paul and means that God declares us guiltless through faith in the work of Christ who bore the full guilt of our sin on the cross for us.

7. The listeners on the first Sabbath were intrigued by Paul's message and were eager to hear more. On the following Sabbath when they saw Gentiles thronging to the synagog, their old prejudice caused them to be seized with jealousy. Jealousy is based on fear, not fact; it refuses to listen to reason. Obviously Paul had a valid message, but the Jews, overcome by jealousy, were predisposed not to listen. Discuss the destructive and irrational nature of this jealousy.

8. Note that the effective preaching of the Word always elicits strong reaction, both positive and negative. Paul and Barnabas spoke so effectively that great numbers believed. Others refused to accept the message, and again persecution was stirred up against the missionaries. Their reaction was not to run away but to spend considerable time in Iconium speaking boldly for the Lord. Opposition was a challenge to them. This encourages us to press on in getting the Word out, despite inevitable resistance and apparent failure.

9. The crowd here was pagan; there were no Jews present. The incident bears out what was observed in lesson 6—all people, even the most primitive, are given a basic knowledge of God through creation. Nevertheless, people are inclined to pervert that knowledge by worshiping the creature rather than the Creator. This was graphically demonstrated in the attempt of the crowd to deify Paul and Barnabas.

10. The same crowd which had sought to worship the missionaries now sought to kill them. This was comparable to Jesus' experiences on Palm Sunday and Good Friday. The same crowd which acclaimed Him as King shouted, "Crucify Him!"

One might well imagine that Paul was remembering his role in the stoning of Stephen.

11. The supreme peril for the Christian worker comes when people suggest he be put on a pedestal. It would have been so easy for Paul and Barnabas to abandon the pathway of persecution and stoning; but the cause of the Kingdom would have suffered immeasurable loss. Can the group think of any current religious leaders whose witness to Christ was diminished or damaged because of notoriety?

12. Circumcision of the Gentiles was the issue. The Judaizers insisted

this was necessary for salvation. Paul and Barnabas saw the grave threat in this teaching. It implied that the work of Christ was not enough to grant salvation but that certain rules and rituals were also necessary. The matter had to be cleared up once and for all if the outreach to the Gentiles was to proceed as God had intended.

Peter recalled God's clear message to him concerning the Gentiles—that they were accepted equally into fellowship with the Jews on the basis of faith alone. Paul and Barnabas reported the work God had been doing among Gentiles through them. James recalled what God had foretold concerning the Gentiles through the prophets.

13. Draw attention to the fact that each of the speakers was seeking to know and to show God's will in the matter. In the end they could report, "It seemed good to the Holy Spirit and to us ..." **(Acts 15:28).**

The church unanimously agreed with the apostle James, who provided leadership for the council. The Gentiles were not to be burdened with Jewish legalism. The four directives involved concerns in which:

a. Gentiles had particular weaknesses (idolatry and adultery).

b. Jews were particularly repulsed (eating strangled meat, which would retain the animal's blood, and eating blood. These were considered human rules, not peculiar to the Jews. See **Gen. 9:4.**)

It would help both the individual and the relationship between Gentile and Jew if these requirements were observed.

14. Paul and Barnabas argued about taking John Mark on the second missionary journey. Even this unhappy circumstance was used by God to multiply the missionary force. There were now two teams: Paul and Silas; Barnabas and Mark.

The Word for Us

1. The Galatian account shows how sharply the issue of Gentile circumcision was debated. Participants should come to see how these leaders were intent on discovering God's will in the issue. To do so, they consulted God's Word (James' contribution) and listened to testimony which revealed the will of God. As they discussed the matter openly, the Holy Spirit led them to a firm conviction of God's intention. If we come to our church meetings prayerfully to study His Word and know His will, we too can come away from them confident that the Holy Spirit is guiding us.

2. John Mark was from Jerusalem. His mother was prominent in the church there and had meetings in her home. Barnabas was his cousin. Mark may have been disturbed when the leadership of the group passed from his cousin to the more forceful Paul. Certainly he was homesick for Jerusalem, and in his youth was not psychologically prepared for the

deprivations and hardships of the journey.

True to his nature, Barnabas, the Son of Encouragement, defended and supported John Mark. Compare **Acts 4:36; 9:27; 11:25.** Ironically, it was he who had promoted Paul's cause before the leaders in Jerusalem when they were suspicious of his sincerity.

Paul, on the other hand, was a man on a mission. In his intensity and commitment to the goal, he could not countenance weakness in himself or in others.

There is a strong and encouraging lesson in the way God ultimately used John Mark to write the gospel of Mark and to be useful in ministry. He doesn't give up on us, and He doesn't cast us aside because of weakness or failure. In His grace He chooses to use us—weak, foolish, self-centered flesh and blood—rather than metal robots which could be programmed for obedience. By His power we are all transformable, redeemable, teachable.

3. Let participants discuss freely here. The point is that many churches, without a clear word from God, have created and elevated inflexible traditions (e.g., the style of building, activities, or program) to a status equal with biblical truth. Form is changeable; biblical truth is unchangeable. To remain spiritually alive, the church may have to adapt its external structure and traditions to meet needs of the people. If society changes, the church will have to be flexible so that it can meet the needs of the people.

4. Paul joyfully embraced opposition and adversity, taking them as a tremendous challenge. For one thing, he realized that the places of persecution and tribulation were the places where he was most needed. Secondly, he realized that these tribulations were a refining process in his personal ministry. When you get into a desperate situation, you begin to realize that self-trust is empty. Confidence toward God generates courage. God gets all the glory. His kingdom is established.

Closing

Sing or speak together the closing hymn.

To Do This Week

Urge participants to complete the suggested activity in preparation for the next class session.

Lesson 8
Nurturing Young Churches
Acts 16–20

Theme Verse
Invite a volunteer to read the theme verse for this lesson.

Goal
Read aloud the goal statement.

What's Going On Here?
Read aloud or have a volunteer read aloud this introductory section.

Searching the Scriptures
1. It is important to work through these items at a fairly steady pace avoiding the temptation to dwell on any one question for a long time. When questions arise which you or someone in the group cannot immediately or satisfactorily answer, jot them down and research them for next time.

2. Assign the places and passages listed to individuals, pairs, or small groups. After a short time have them report their answers.

3. Paul was not making concessions to the Judaizers. Timothy's ministry would be expedited and broadened by this measure. Paul wanted to win the Jews over, not turn them away offended. The Corinthians passage should be read aloud to shed light on Paul's attitude.

4. This question reinforces a principle which has been demonstrated repeatedly in Acts: God the Holy Spirit governs the forward movement of the church. God promises to speak to us through His Word. The Holy Spirit is poured out on us in Baptism, and our faith is strengthened by our Lord's Supper. The Spirit leads the church today by guiding our common sense, reason, and wisdom gained from experience.

5. Luke apparently joined the group in Troas, probably stayed in Philippi when Paul left, and rejoined him, upon his return.

6. Throughout the study we have observed variant receptions to the Gospel. The Athenians present a new attitude. Their example reminds us that God has given His Word, not to satisfy our curiosity, but to change our lives. How is this truth demonstrated in the example of the jailer? Ask the group if they can identify similar reactions to the Gospel message today.

7. It is amazing that Paul and Silas could sing hymns of praise and ado-

ration in such miserable and painful circumstances. Have participants identify a problem in their lives. Challenge them to offer God praise in these situations, not as a matter of feeling but of obedience. How can we thank God in every situation? Remind participants that only by the power of the Holy Spirit working through God's Word to strengthen our faith can we thank God in all circumstances.

8. The Bereans were not commended for naively saying yes to the interpretation of the preacher, but rather for appealing again and again to Scripture as the final authority. How does this passage encourage you?

9. We can all relate to Paul who must certainly have been at a point similar to burn out. It reminds us of Elijah who, after a great spiritual victory over the prophets of Baal, became fearful of Jezebel and fell into depression. How kind of God to include such examples so that we may understand that we need not be superhuman to serve Him.

10. By way of background you may draw attention to the fact that Paul spent some time in Antioch (18:23) between the two journeys.

Use this item simply to review the areas of the work. Rather than moving from place to place Paul remained for a time in Ephesus perhaps making excursions into the surrounding district of West Asia Minor.

11. The Ephesian disciples were unaware that the Holy Spirit had been given to the church, the new people of God. They knew John's baptism to be the baptism of promise. Baptism in the name of Jesus is the Baptism of fulfillment. Paul wanted the Ephesians to receive the full blessing of God's Spirit through faith in Christ.

Note that Apollos is not in Ephesus at this point. Aquila and Priscilla have already helped him come to the full light of faith in Christ, and he is at this moment ministering in Corinth.

12. Observe that it was the believers in Ephesus who came and confessed their evil deeds. They had come to faith in Christ but had apparently retained some of the trappings of the occult which were so prevalent in Ephesian society. There is room for soul-searching here. Many Christians attempt to retain old ungodly habits after receiving Christ. Read **1 John 1:9.** Remind participants that God's great love for us in Christ Jesus motivates and empowers us to do that which God desires.

13. When Jesus healed the demon-possessed man and sent the "Legion" into the herd of swine, the pagans in the area were more concerned about the financial loss of the pigs than about knowing the One who could heal illnesses. Similarly in these accounts the pagans are concerned about losing their source of income (fortune-telling, the idol-making industry). This blinds them to the truth which is being demonstrated in the life-changing Gospel.

Many Jews, on the other hand, rejected the truth out of self-righteous prejudice and pride. This made them equally closed to God's revelation of mercy in Christ.

14. Note these aspects of an early church meeting. Have members compare them with their personal experience in church fellowship: an intimate meeting in a private home; celebration of the Lord's Supper; the centrality of teaching; a preacher available to share concerns; listeners hungry for the Word and Sacrament. Church buildings were not constructed until the third century.

It was quite natural, considering the small room, the many lamps, and the late hour, for the lad Eutychus to fall asleep. Like Elijah and Elisha (**1 Kings 17:21; 2 Kings 4:34**), Paul stretched himself over the youth, and by the power of God his life was restored.

15. False teachers were the greatest threat to the church and still are. Have participants observe the texts cited and reserve discussion for the "The Word for Us" section.

16. Assign passages to individuals or groups. While they are looking for answers, you may look up **1 Thess. 2:7–12**. After answers have been reported, read this passage to the group. It sums up beautifully Paul's attitude toward the churches he had planted.

The Word for Us

1. Through these studies participants should be developing a growing awareness of their personal responsibility to the health of the church. Aquila and Priscilla are prime examples of what it means to be involved in body life. If the church appears to be maimed and crippled, it is because we aren't functioning as a body, with each member doing his or her part.

Many of us are low-functioning members, that is, our church life consists only of going to church on Sunday, merely sitting down and thinking, "God, it's good to be here." Low-functioning members retard the growth, maturity, and witness of the church. God calls us to serve one another with the spiritual gifts He has given us. If we don't minister to one another, we cannot grow.

2. The purpose of this question is to help participants come to some personal understanding of what constitutes a false teacher. False teachers are a very real threat in the church today. Help participants see from the texts that the two ingredients necessary to combat false teaching are:

a. *A living relationship with God through Jesus Christ.* If we really know Christ and live in a moment-by-moment relationship with Him ("walking in the Spirit"), we are unlikely to submit to teachings which ignore Christ, misrepresent Him, or replace Him with a person or idol.

b. *Staying in the Word.* The Word is the sword with which we can cut down Satan's lies. That is why we study as we do now and memorize Scripture.

3. Have volunteers look up and read aloud the texts one after the other. Remind participants that we want to be persistent in the things to which *God* has called us. We cannot individually answer every need we discover. We can trust that God will accomplish His will through others as well as through us. By keeping in touch with God through the study of His Word and prayer, we will come to know which tasks He has for us. This will keep us from the pitfall of spreading ourselves too thin.

4. This question brings the whole point of the lesson to bear upon each of us personally. Loving Christ means willingness to serve His church. As sinners, we confess that we are guilty of unfaithfulness, carnality, self-centeredness, pride, divisiveness, and spiritual laziness. As saints, by faith in Christ, we trust the Holy Spirit to bring our lives into conformity with Christ Jesus, giving us the energy to serve Him unselfishly.

Closing

Speak or sing together the closing hymn.

To Do This Week

Urge participants to complete the suggested activities.

Lesson 9

Bound and Yet Free

Acts 21–24

Theme Verse

Invite a volunteer to read the theme verse for this lesson.

Goal

Read aloud the goal statement.

What's Going On Here?

Read aloud or have a volunteer read aloud this introductory section.

Searching the Scriptures

1. Ideally each member has read through the chapters under discussion prior to meeting. Review the sequence of events by way of introduction: Paul returns to Jerusalem and reports to the elders; he falls into the hands of the Jewish mob; he is arrested by the Romans; he addresses the mob; he is given a hearing before the Sanhedrin; he is secreted away to Caesarea; he stands trial before the governor Felix.

2. The tenderness and warmth expressed in these scenes are reminiscent of the final topics of study in lesson 8.

3. Work through the questions together and then discuss how to deal with opposing opinions concerning God's will. When the believers released Paul with the words "The Lord's will be done," they indicated that they had come to agree with Paul in his understanding of the Lord's will.

The test of motive should always be applied when such questions are being considered: "Am I doing this for my sake or to fulfill God's purposes?"

4. This visit to Jerusalem took place some 20 years after the birth of the church on Pentecost. It is distressing to observe that this mother church had become accustomed to concession and to compromise. Note that Paul was being urged to accommodate himself to Jewish believers who should be free from the external rituals of Judaism, but who instead retained these old forms while professing faith in Christ. The result was a weakened local church. This congregation, which had always been cool toward Paul and his outreach to the Gentiles, provided no aid when he was attacked by the Jewish mob.

5. Paul's deep love for the Jewish nation and his longing that his kinsmen turn to the light of Christ never wavered. According to the Romans passage, he almost would be willing to sacrifice his own salvation to see this desire fulfilled.

6. We see once again how blind and irrational was the prejudice of the Jews against the Gentiles. The crowd listened attentively until the hated name of Gentile was mentioned.

7. Martyrdom is only of value when it cannot be avoided. Paul had just been violently beaten; a flogging at this point might well have meant death. This argues against seeking to suffer for the sake of suffering.

8. It is gracious of God to include this incident and to show that Paul was by no means a plastic Christian. Yet notice how quickly he retracted the sharp remark in deference to God's Word (**Ex. 22:28**). By admitting his fault and conforming to the Scriptural principle without hesitation, he exhibited rare humility and self-control.

9. Jesus' trial, as well as that of Peter and John, before this same assem-

bly proved that these religious leaders were hardened to the truth. They were ruthless and inflexible, using all forms of corruption to achieve their own ends. Paul was wise to elude their grasp by pitting the Sadducees against the Pharisees.

10. The darkness seems to have fallen around Paul. He was used to beatings and imprisonments; his concern was not for his own life. The dejection reflected apparent failure in the Lord's work. Paul had accommodated the Jewish Christians, but to no avail; a riot ensued. He had seized the opportunity to give testimony to his Jewish brothers which only infuriated them more. The church in Jerusalem stood aloof. Only the Roman commander seems to have had any feeling for Paul's plight.

We know what Paul's state of mind must have been, because of the Lord's gracious words "Take courage." He then encouraged Paul concerning what he had done in Jerusalem and showed him that this was all part of God's own plan to bring him, as His witness, to Rome.

11. God often chooses the most illogical or mundane things to provide for and protect his servants. Here it was a Roman commander and a young lad. God is not limited; He can use anything and anyone to achieve His purposes. Not only did He remove Paul from the dangerous situation, He provided the comfort of a horse and the protection of 470 soldiers! When he was delivered safely to Caesarea, he was quartered in a palace!

12. Assign passages of Paul's defense to participants. As the charges are read from the study guide, have the corresponding defense read from the Bible. Notice how composed Paul was. This was the result of the Lord's appearing.

By adjourning the proceedings, Felix was deciding in Paul's favor. Lysias, the commander, never did come.

13. Do not neglect to look up the passage in **1 Peter.** It is a clear statement of how Christians should view life and conduct themselves while here on earth.

14. Awareness of sin is the first step toward repentance and redemption. The sensation of fear and trembling is a gracious emotion, if it leads to faith. If Felix had but climbed from fear to faith! Instead, he postponed the issue.

15. Joseph, like Paul, was in prison for two years. The story of both men shows that God can use even our prison experiences to accomplish His purposes. Joseph, ever faithful to God, ministered where he was, found favor in the sight of his fellow prisoners and superiors, and was eventually promoted to second ruler in the kingdom. Paul used his imprisonment as an opportunity to witness, and he received a much-needed two-year rest in comparative comfort.

The Word for Us

1. Personal testimony and the experience of the believer prepare the way for witness. They never take the place of preaching the life, death, and resurrection of Christ, but they catch the attention of the listener. It is not enough, for example, to tell how much your church affiliation means to you. This should be a springboard to telling of Christ and what He has done to save us. Jesus Christ is always the topic of our confession of faith.

2. Trembling at one's sin is an opportunity to turn to God. Instead of casting himself immediately upon God's mercy, Felix vacillated and postponed the decision. The result was a hardened heart. We do not know for sure that Felix was not eventually saved. It is clear that Paul never failed to deliver the message of salvation. This should give encouragement to anyone who has labored in witness and prayer to lead another to Christ with no apparent results.

Direct participants to pause at this time and call to mind someone they have tried to win to Christ without success. Tell them to use this opportunity to recommit the matter to God and to renew their commitment to pray for and witness to this person.

3. Christianity often is challenged, because its leaders, who are in the public eye, do not maintain a holy walk. Open up discussion on this point. How can we help our leaders? What is the responsibility of each Christian regarding personal holiness? By whose power alone can we remain pure? See **Zech. 4:6b.**

4. We avail ourselves to God's nearness through His Word. Participants will probably have little problem coming up with passages which assure us of God's continued presence with us (e.g., **Ps. 46:1, Deut. 31:6, Matt. 28:20b**). Nevertheless, there is probably an area in the life of each individual present where it seems as if the Lord has withdrawn His presence or is somehow not in control. Have members promise to pray daily about this matter; whenever it comes to mind, they should turn it over to the Lord, thanking Him that He is in control. Each time they are inclined to worry, they should turn the worry into a prayer. Give them **Phil. 4:6–7** as a Scriptural basis for this. Encourage them to look up that passage and think about it frequently as they pray about their situation repeatedly to the Lord.

Closing

Sing or speak together the closing hymn stanza.

To Do This Week

Urge participants to complete the suggested activity prior to the next class session.

Lesson 10

The Church Prevails

Acts 25–28

Theme Verse

Invite a volunteer to read the theme verse for this lesson.

Goal

Read aloud the goal statement.

What's Going On Here?

Read aloud or have a volunteer read aloud this introductory section.

Searching the Scriptures

1. You may at this point refresh participants' memories by giving a quick summary of these last four chapters in **Acts: 25**—Paul's case reviewed by Festus; Paul's appeal to Rome; **26**—the hearing before Agrippa; **27**—voyage to Rome and storm at sea; **28**—continued work of evangelization while Paul is kept under house arrest in Rome.

2. In order to escape the murderous hatred of his countrymen, Paul was forced to appeal to Caesar, the highest court of appeal in the Roman legal system. All along God has used Rome to protect Paul from the Jews. These experiences undoubtedly influenced Paul's portrait of secular government in **Rom. 13:1–7** where he describes the political authorities as "God's servant to do you good."

3. Festus is at a loss to specify the charges against Paul. He hoped that Agrippa, who was acquainted with Jewish beliefs, would help him clarify the matter. Festus took special care to be just and conscientious in the administration of his office.

4. Take time to have volunteers read each of the three accounts. In chapter 26 Paul was more specific about the commission the Lord gave to him **(v. 18)**. He was speaking, not to a crowd, but to an individual, and he tried to gain Agrippa's heart for Christ by incorporating the Gospel message into his personal testimony.

5. Group members may be able to recount times when they have been regarded as crazy for witnessing boldly to Christ. It should encourage them to know that they are in good company. **1 Cor. 1:18–25** which concerns God's "foolishness" in Christ is another supportive passage on this issue.

Others, like Agrippa, will procrastinate. Paul never gave up in his witness, nor should we.

6. Recall how, after the Lord's appearing in the Roman barracks at Jerusalem, Paul never again wavered in the conviction that God would accomplish His purposes in him by bringing him to Rome. After that nighttime visit, Paul moved quietly and strongly toward the goal, superior to all circumstances, yet all the time buying up the opportunities.

7. This is a fine example of Luke's narrative skills; it reads like *Moby Dick*. Observe the nautical details. Allow free discussion.

8. Paul was living in fellowship with God. He was safer on a storm-tossed sea, living in the will of God, than if he was resting comfortably at home, living disobediently outside the will of God.

9. Contrast the unreliability of people with the total reliability of God. People demonstrate their fickle nature, shouting one moment, "He is a murderer!" and the next, "He is a god!" We may, however, confidently place our trust in God and never be disappointed.

10. Based on the text, Paul's ministry was principally one of healing. Undoubtedly he shared the Gospel too. This would have been of particular interest to the physician Luke.

11. Paul first ministers to his Jewish brethren, and predictably, upon their rejection, turns to the Gentiles.

12. From beginning to end, Jesus Christ is the center of this account as He should be of all the church's doings and of our individual lives. See **Heb. 12:2–3.**

The Word for Us

1. **Psalm 107** has many rich lessons concerning the ravages of life—the dry and empty times, the times of bondage and despair, the times of debilitating illness, the stormy times. In each instance the psalmist enjoins us to seek deliverance from God and then to "give thanks to the Lord for His unfailing love and his wonderful deeds for men."

Paul, as a well-educated Hebrew, knew this familiar psalm and acted through faith in accordance with it.

2. You planted the seed of thought for this item at the beginning of the session. There should be a growing awareness of the similarities between Paul's journey and our own lives. Discuss the assurances we receive from the outcome of the voyage.

3. Work through this question together. For example, God does want us to build our homes and families, but not as an end in themselves. We are to love our husband or wife, nurture our children, and keep our homes for Him; all should be set apart for His use and His glory.

It is a sad fact that many Christians see this life as an opportunity for self-aggrandizement and self-indulgence. Suggest that if God had left us here after our salvation to live comfortable lives, He would have done better to take us directly to heaven, where comforts abound. The question really is "Why did God leave us on earth after He saved?"

4. This is a good wrap-up for lesson 10 and for the entire study. It should generate ample discussion. Remind the group that as we continue to study God's Word, He will reveal His purposes in our lives, although it may be difficult at times to discern His directions for this life.

Closing

Invite a volunteer to read aloud the introductory paragraphs. Sing or speak together the closing hymn.